The Private Sector After Communism

The transformation of state-owned enterprises into privately owned ones is commonly referred to as 'privatization'. Just as important as this process, though sometimes not given the attention it deserves and requires, is the establishment and expansion of new private firms.

This book analyzes new entrepreneurial firms that emerge and occasionally flourish after a period of state communism has come to an end. The authors rightly focus on the aftermath of the end of communism by looking first at the inevitable output decline, followed by an overview of new entrepreneurial firms. Specific East European examples are examined and the lessons which can be learned from these will interest academics and policy-makers alike.

Committed and knowledgeable authors in this book treat the sometimes emotive issue of transition-developing economies maturely and expertly. The result is a volume which will interest scholars with an interest in transition economics and politics, as well as those who actively work in transition economies.

Jan Winiecki is Professor and Chair, International Economics and European Integration, University of Computer Science and Management, Rzeszow, Poland.

Vladimir Benacek is at present with the Economic Commission for Europe. He is affiliated with the Charles University, Prague.

Mihaly Laki is Visiting Associate Professor of Political Science at the Central European University, Budapest, and researcher at the Institute of Economics, also in Budapest, Hungary.

Routledge studies in development economics

The Private Sector After Communism

New entrepreneurial firms in transition economies

Jan Winiecki, Vladimir Benacek and Mihaly Laki

Routledge
Taylor & Francis Group

LONDON AND NEW YORK

First published 2004
by Routledge
2 Park Square, Milton Park, Abingdon,
Oxfordshire OX14 4RN

Simultaneously published in the USA and Canada
by Routledge
29 West 35th Street, New York, NY 10001

Routledge is an imprint of the Taylor & Francis Group

© 2004 Jan Winiecki, Vladimir Benacek and Mihaly Laki

Typeset in Times by
Keystroke, Jacaranda Lodge, Wolverhampton

Printed and bound in Great Britain by
TJ International Ltd, Padstow, Cornwall

British Library Cataloguing in Publication Data
A catalogue record for this book is available from
the British Library

Library of Congress Cataloging in Publication Data
A catalog record for this book has been requested

ISBN 0–415–31807–6

Contents

Figures

Tables

Introduction

The natural effort of every individual to better his own condition . . . is so powerful a principle, that it is alone . . . not only capable of carrying on the society to wealth and prosperity, but of surmounting a hundred impertinent obstructions, with which the folly of human laws too often encumbers its operations.

(Adam Smith, *The Wealth of Nations*, Liberty Classics edition, 1976)

This book is yet another story of post-communist transformation (or transition, or systemic change – all terms are intended to mean the same and are used interchangeably). But it is one that is rarely told from the perspective taken here. For it makes the *new private firms* the centerpiece of the story. Their establishment and expansion, their share in the aggregate output and employment, and the enabling conditions required for their success, are shown to be of crucial importance for the transition process.

Most of the literature dealing with the emergence and role of the private sector in post-communist transition concentrates on what is commonly called privatization. But what the authors usually mean by the term in question is the transformation of state-owned enterprises into privately owned ones. What they tend to often forget is that the private sector in post-communist economies is created *via* two parallel processes. Another process, alongside the ownership transformation, is the establishment and expansion of new private firms.

The author of this Introduction suggested more than a decade ago that both processes are two sides of the same story of privatization, that is the creation of the dominant private sector in national economies of post-communist countries (see Gruszecki and Winiecki, 1991, and Winiecki, 1992). While both contribute to the growth of the private sector, they differ by their respective institutional characteristics. The ownership transformation, called privatization "from above", requires much more state activism than the establishment and expansion of new private firms.

Those researchers who concentrated on the privatization "from above" have been following the pattern set at the very start of transition, when politicians, pundits, and the general public pinned their transition hopes on state-owned enterprises (SOEs for short) and their change into efficient private firms. Yet they were by and large *justified* in their concentration on SOEs (and state controlled pseudo-cooperatives) inherited from the communist past. After all, those old firms employed at the start in between 80 percent and 100 percent of the total labor force in the enterprise sector and produced a corresponding share of output. In the emerging democracies the concerns of the majority could not be neglected.

It is easy to notice a limited vision of things to come displayed by those elaborating transition programs, or what the author calls the "Holy Trinity" of transition: stabilization, liberalization, and privatization. In the first public presentation of the outline of Polish program of systemic change (in October 1989), the role of new private firms had been treated in a highly perfunctory manner. In barely half a sentence the program promised to create conditions of "full freedom to establish new firms." The reader should note that the adjective "private" did not appear in the program outline (more about specifically Polish problems in Chapter 5).

Clearly, politicians, pundits, and the public were concentrating on what was easily observable, that is on the (overwhelmingly) large state enterprises. And yet, it should have been clear – at least for policy-makers and pundits – that SOEs employed much too much labor at a given level of output. Moreover, an unknown, but undoubtedly large, part of their output was what in communist times was called "production for production's sake." Demand for such "pure socialist production," according to the apt expression of Leszek Balcerowicz, should have been expected to disappear, together with the disappearance of the system that generated such wasteful production.

Consequently, labor disgorged by state mastodons, all those hundreds of thousands of employees, would be expected to find employment somewhere else. Employment in the traditional public (non-enterprise) sector apart, they would have to find it in the production of goods and services. And the foregoing meant that they would be looking for employment in the new private firms, treated so perfunctorily by the architects of transition. There was no third way (there usually is not, in spite of the longings of many!).

It is, of course, tempting to interpret the neglect by reference to the introductory quote from Adam Smith about individuals' propensity to better their lot as a powerful motive to perform. But if the ruling elites adopted, indeed, the Smithian perspective, then we are justified in expecting to see more extensive proposals to remove the "impertinent obstacles" of communist regulatory inheritance that stifled initiative and distorted the behavior of economic agents. Half a sentence, we read above, was certainly not enough. And non-communist regulatory regimes differ, too, offering a range of choices. If Canadian rules of establishment entail two procedures, while French require *sixteen* (see, Djankov *et al.*, 2000), there is a wide range of alternative arrangements to be adopted!

A much more realistic interpretation, however, of the perfunctory treatment of the conditions of establishment and operation of the enterprise sector was a combination of ignorance, probably inevitable at the start, and political calculus. The first is self-explanatory, the second is explainable by the large numbers' law of mathematics. The large numbers of employees and, by the same token, of electoral votes were associated with SOEs and it is to these large numbers employed in SOEs and, increasingly (albeit slowly), privatized ex-SOEs that the governments, coping with the plethora of transition-related issues, allocated their scarce resources – time and money.

However, what is understandable in the case of policy-makers, the general public, and even more so those from the public directly affected by the fate of their enterprises, is less understandable in the case of researchers. For they knew, or at least should have known, what we wrote earlier, namely that output and employment in the state enterprises would have to be sharply reduced if privatized and restructured SOEs were ever to compete successfully on equal footing with other firms (domestic and foreign). For them it should have been clearer that the only hope for employment of those made redundant in the old state enterprise sector was new private firms, first of all domestic and later – as the dust settled – also foreign ones.

Be that as it may, neither the literature on general characteristics of transition, nor the more specific one on the new private sector (usually, for statistical convenience, equated with the small and medium-sized firms) have devoted much consideration to the crucial role of the new private firms. The foregoing dictum applied to both transformational recession (as defined by Janos Kornai) and to transformational recovery.

In the case of transformational recession, new private firms were conspicuous by their very limited impact upon the output path in the early period of post-communist transition. However fast they grew (see Part II, Chapters 3–5 of this book), their starting point was too low, in terms of output and employment, to cushion the very large fall of output in state enterprises. The fall in question, so hotly criticized by many in early transition, has been an inevitable correction of the distorted pattern of economic activity under the communist economic system (see, i.a., Winiecki, 1988).

Given the very large size of the correction, additions of the new private sector to aggregate output were far too small in the first years to significantly reduce the subtractions from it due to falling demand and output of SOEs and ex-SOEs. For privatized ex-SOEs were in the first years after privatization in a roughly similar situation to state firms: restructuring inevitably entailed output cuts and employment cuts (the latter usually with a lag). More on that in Part I, Chapter 2 below.

In the case of transformational recovery it has not often been stressed in the literature that the very occurrence of the recovery in the short to medium run perspective on transition (three to seven years) was wholly dependent on the dynamics of the new private sector. Wherever institutional framework has been conducive for the expansion of new private firms, relatively early recovery from transformational recession became a fact. Where the frame-work in question was weak, flawed, or next to non-existent, recovery did not occur. Output continued to decline for years in a row.

The story briefly sketched above is told in much greater detail in Part I of the book. Chapter 1 has been devoted to transformational recession. First the universal pattern of the output fall is presented, its universality independent of the speed or consistency of the respective transition programs (or even their absence). Next, the distorted structure of incentives under the old system is revealed to suggest where output fall would come from, given the responses of SOEs to the new structure of incentives, set at the start of transition to the market. Then, actual pattern of output fall is confronted with the communist legacy-based expectations; the concordance between the two is clearly visible.

If in Chapter 1 we deal with determinants of output fall, than in Chapter 2 we concentrate on determinants of output recovery. Therefore, there is a shift of primary attention from the old state sector, inherited from the past, to the new private sector, emerging after the start of transition. The latter sector, too small in early years to influence decisively the pattern of output, begins to add more and more to output in successful transition economies. At a certain point of time its positive net contribution to aggregate output exceeds negative net contribution of SOEs and privatized ex-SOEs. At that point transformational recession ends and transformational recovery begins.

Chapter 2 begins with the overview of the economic and non-economic importance of new, entrepreneurial sector (which, given the scarcity of data, is most often measured by proxy as the SME sector). Next, alternative scenarios are drawn. Early recovery is linked to the dynamic expansion of the new private sector, while the lack of it is seen as primarily the consequence of the unsuccessful or less successful expansion of the new private sector.

Then, comes the important part of the chapter, where determinants of success or failure are considered at length. Explanations there differ markedly from those traditionally offered in the transition literature. The author looks in Chapter 2 beyond the specific rules of the establishment and operations of the enterprise sector and even beyond the general rules of transition (the already mentioned "Holy Trinity" of transition). Important as they both are, they nonetheless are seen to have less impact upon success or failure than have the civilizational fundamentals of political liberty, law and order, and general trust (social capital). Their presence or absence, or to be more precise, their greater or smaller presence, is crucial for the expansion of the new private firms. These fundamentals are basically derived from the pre-communist history of each country undergoing systemic change. Thus, history casts a long shadow, affecting transition's success or failure.

Part I sets the pattern of both transformational recession and recovery, and the role of the new private sector in that pattern. In turn, Part II offers supporting evidence on the new private sector in three countries, commonly regarded as success stories of both transition in general and the expansion of the new private sector in particular: the Czech Republic, Hungary, and Poland. As the reader will undoubtedly note, each country's story is somewhat different. Numerous similarities are interspersed with some differences. Take, for example, the privatization "from above" and its impact on the evolving structure of the aggregate private sector.

The Czechs (see Chapter 3 by Vladimir Benacek) have gone their own way in this respect. Citizens' privatization (*kuponovka*) helped to move away fast from state ownership, but then encountered difficulties as further changes in the structure of ownership were blocked by the unfinished reforms of the financial sector. Little strategic ownership by specialized investors emerged as a result. The Hungarians (see Chapter 4 by Mihaly Laky) pursued doggedly their basic strategy of selling to the highest bidder. They were kept on that virtuous path by the insatiable appetite for revenues by the expanding state budget. The Poles (see Chapter 5 by Jan Winiecki) fell somewhere in between, with their compromises on both limited citizens' privatization and strong pressure for insiders' privatization (primarily employee ownership). What set Poland somewhat apart was stronger resistance to *any* privatization than in the Czech Republic or Hungary. Interestingly, stronger resistance to privatization "from above" in Poland, which made the privatized sector smaller, created *greater* room for expansion for new private firms.

But regardless of occasional differences, the (generally positive) outcomes with respect to the dynamics of the new private firms were roughly similar. The impact of the new private sector has been very strong, with its share reaching 40–50 percent GDP, or even more, within less than a decade. Clearly, similarities were stronger than differences: primarily the civilizational fundamentals.

Some differences resulted from variations in economic history under communism. For example, the private sector was completely eliminated in the former Czechoslovakia. In Hungary and Poland, policy twists and turns apart, it was marginalized, but allowed to survive. An interesting observation concerning the latter two countries can be made on the basis of Chapters 4 and 5. Namely, the *old* private sector, i.e. private firms established under the communist system, did not flourish during the post-communist shift to the market.

Old private firms failed as often as old SOEs (and old *pseudo*-cooperatives). The corrosive legacy of the past patterns of low quality, the lack of innovative spirit, excessive investment, etc., made old private firms as unfit to compete successfully on the market as old SOEs. Therefore, the alleged advantage of Hungary and Poland over the Czech Republic and other post-communist economies, seen in having the private sector already at the start of transition, seems to be dubious at best. The similarity of outcomes suggests that other determinants were much more important.

As the civilizational fundamentals have been on the whole propitious in the case of the three East-Central European countries considered at some length in Part II of this book, both institutional developments and economic outcomes turned out to be basically similar. The institutional side of the story suggests that problems encountered by new private firms in their operations were similar across the board. In fact various survey studies quoted in country chapters suggest that the problems were similar also in other countries, not only those belonging to the group of transition leaders.

Unsurprisingly, the two most often stressed types of barriers concerned regulatory regimes and taxes. Complaints about the regulatory regimes stressed invariably the rapidity of change in the rules, their inconsistency, lack of transparency, and arbitrariness of applications by the bureaucracy. Part of the complaints is explainable in terms of the legal overhaul to be done in a country undergoing systemic change; part is not. The latter is a signal that the bureaucracy, as well as the political class, try to increase their control over the spontaneous economic processes for political and material gains.

Complaints on the inconsistency and non-transparency of tax rules, as well as on the arbitrariness of tax authorities, have the same origins as above. Complaints, however, on the *level* of taxes have a different rationale. It is well known that small and medium-sized firms finance most of their expansion from their firms' profits. High corporate and personal income tax rates create obstacles to expansion in the face of a more difficult access to external financing than in stable market economies. With little or no accumulated capital before the start of transition, high profitability and low taxes are the best prescription for expansion. Therefrom stems the growing popularity of a linear (flat rate) tax in post-communist economies in the last years.

Part II of the book offers another interesting lesson about the relative unimportance of state activism going beyond the creation of the conducive general framework of transition. Of the three countries in question Hungary has been seen as the most persistent tinkerer in the area of specific institutional support for the SME sector expansion. And yet there are no significant differences between Hungary on the one hand and the Czech Republic and Poland on the other, in terms of outcomes. Clearly, the Smithian removal of "impertinent obstructions" and the existence of civilizational similarities (*vis-à-vis*, for example, Russia) had more influence on the expansion of the private sector. The foregoing offers strong support for the Chapter 2 generalizations on the determinants of success or failure in the establishment and expansion of the new private sector.

Toward the end of this Introduction it is time for acknowledgements. Certainly the greatest debt the authors owe to the Earhart Foundation and personally to its President Dave Kennedy. It is his interest in a paper presented by Jan Winiecki at a Mont Pelerin Society meeting at Potsdam (Germany) in October 1999 that started the whole effort. A grant from the Earhart Foundation allowed authors to concentrate more on the subject in question, while the research report from the project caught attention of Routledge editors. The usual disclaimers, however, apply.

The writer of this Introduction has acknowledgments of his own. First he would like to thank Professor Pekka Sutela, the director of the Bank of Finland Institute of Transformation for the invitation to join the team there. Consequently, I spent two months in the friendly and intellectually stimulating atmosphere in the summer of 2001. The paper written during that stay formed the basis of Chapter 2 of this book. Finally, I would like to thank the editor of *Post-Communist Economies* and their publisher, Carfax, for the permission to use the article on output fall in early transition, published in Vol. 14, No. 1, 2002, as a basis of Chapter 1. Also, I would like to thank the editor of *Europe-Asia*, and the same publisher, for the permission to use the article on the Polish generic private sector in transition, published in vol. 54, No. 1, 2002.

Part I
Old and new firms in decline and recovery

1 Transformational recession

Impact on the old state sector

Jan Winiecki

Introduction

The major fall of output in early transition from communist centrally planned to capitalist market economy became an issue very early in the transition process. The Polish economy, that began its transition program the earliest, that is on January 1, 1990, registered what at that time looked like a shockingly large output decline. Thus, industrial output fell by about 25 percent and GDP by 12 percent in 1990. It fell some more next year.

Critics of transition censured the fall as "the unbearable cost of transition." Subsequently, it became a rallying cry of all those suspicious of or hostile to the market. "Big bang" (or "shock therapy" as the transition program was then called) was accused of generating a depression of unprecedented proportions – and an avoidable depression at that (see, e.g., Laski, 1990, and Bhaduri and Laski, 1992). Some analysts regarded the Polish and Czech big bang, that is a large package of measures, as *the* culprit and contrasted that with the allegedly different – and more successful – gradual transition in Hungary (see, e.g., Dervis and Condon, 1994). However, already in the same year of 1992 it transpired that there was little difference in the aggregate output numbers between Poland, Hungary, and Czechoslovakia.

A year later, in 1993, one of the keenest observers of the scene at the time, Kornai (1993), noted that that output declined everywhere: in big bang countries and in "gradualist" countries, in internationally indebted countries and in debt-free countries like the former Czechoslovakia, in countries consistently following the transition program and in those that did not. Figure 1.1A and 1.1B (from Blanchard, 1997), reflects this observation very well as it shows the almost identical pattern of output fall, measured in years from the beginning of the transition program (not in calendar years). It is worth noting that the very large output fall also affected countries that did not follow *any* transition program (such as, e.g., Ukraine).

Industrial statistics of post-communist countries reveal that in the early transition, or "transformational recession" (Kornai's expression reflecting

A. Pattern of GDP volume change   **B. Pattern of industrial output volume change**

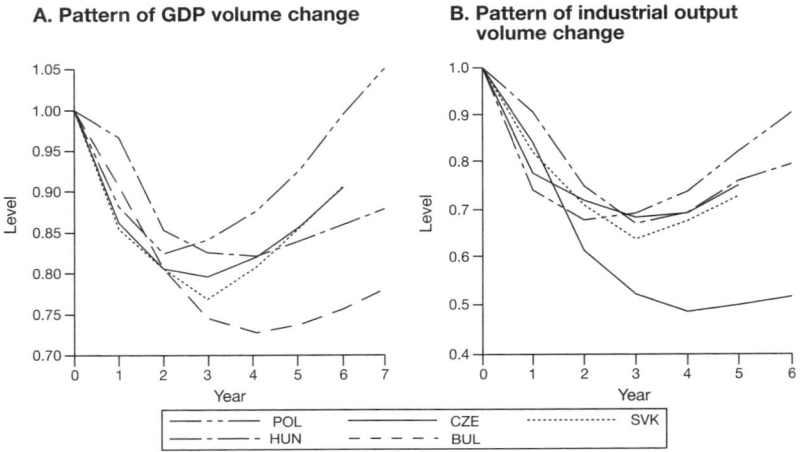

Figure 1.1 Pattern of GDP and industrial output in East-Central Europe volume change in transition.

Note: Value in the year before transition = 1.0.
Source: Blanchard, 1997.

the process of removing various structural distortions), or elimination of "pure socialist production" not needed under normal circumstances (L. Balcerowicz, 1995), output declines were very large everywhere. The data for the first three to four years of transition, concerning industrial output, confirm the pattern from Figure 1.1 for a larger number of East-Central European and East European countries (see Table 1.1).

Consequently, the accusations about the "cruelty" of shock therapy subsided somewhat and a near-consensus view emerged that output fall at the start of transition was all but unavoidable (for a good summary, see Csaba, 1998). Kornai's definition of "transformational recession" has been widely accepted. Of course, not everybody agreed. Every now and then one hears voices of unrepentant accusers. Those who dislike transition, more precisely the *direction* of change, have an obvious interest in repeating the baseless accusations *ad nauseam*. After all, the propaganda rules apply here as well. If you repeat the untruth often enough it may continue to compete with truth for the attention of some readers. Curiously, however, although analysts largely agreed on basic facts, they nonetheless "agreed to disagree" on their causes. A range of views has been formulated as to the causes of such a very large output fall – and these views differed sharply.

Table 1.1 Aggregate industrial output fall in selected post-communist countries of East-Central and Eastern Europe (calculated from the start of transition)

Country	Years	Output change %
Bulgaria	1991–93	–41.3
Czech Republic	1991–93	–31.3
Hungary	1990–92	–30.7
Poland	1990–92	–28.3
Romania	1991–94	–36.9
Lithuania	1992–94	–60.2
Belarus	1992–95	–32.0
Russia	1992–95	–46.1
Ukraine	1992–95	–44.7

Sources: *Countries in Transition, 1999*, by the Vienna Institute for International Economic Studies, Vienna; *Transition Report, 1996*, by the European Bank for Reconstruction and Development, London; *Statistical Yearbook, 1998*, Central Statistical Office of Poland, Warsaw.

Note: No data are available for industrial production in early 1990s for Estonia, Latvia, and Moldova. Post-communist Yugoslav countries, as well as Armenia, Georgia, and Azerbaijan have not been included due to the additional impact of civil war on the pattern and level of output.

However, with transition moving, at least in "success stories," from the phase of transformational recession to recovery, the theoretical debate shifted from causes of output fall to causes of output recovery (or the lack of it), and theoretical considerations about the former subsided as well. The latter story is analyzed in detail in Chapter 2. Therefore, I would like to continue here with the early phase of output fall. The debate on its causes, stressed above, subsided on a note of complete disagreement. Whenever the issue has been broached in later considerations, the views from early transition were simply presented again, without much added reflection on the subject (compare, e.g., Gomulka, 1991 and 1998).

However, such "agreement on disagreement" is intellectually highly unsatisfactory. After all, this has been a – if not the – major theoretical puzzle of early transition (see, e.g., Winiecki, 2000a). Stabilization *cum* liberalization outside the post-communist world usually entailed a relatively limited output loss, or, under certain circumstances, even slight output increase. Leaving unsolved the puzzle of a very large output fall in the case of post-communist economies undergoing similar process suggests a major weakness in theorizing on the economics of transition.

Moreover, not only shock therapy (or "big bang") offered little support for the view stressing its role as the major determinant of output fall, but also initial conditions as debated at the time (see, e.g., Fischer and Gelb, 1991) did not do any better in this respect. Post-communist countries differed among

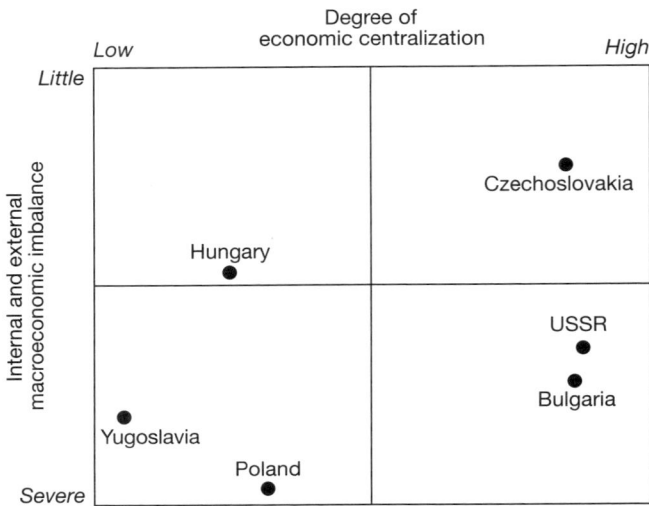

Figure 1.2 Initial conditions in post-communist economies.
Source: S. Fischer and A. Gelb, 1991: 91–105.

themselves with respect to the degree of economic centralization and initial macroeconomic imbalance, as shown in Figure 1.2 (adapted from Fischer and Gelb), but again this differentiation did not offer us any clue as to the cause (or causes) of a very large output fall everywhere, regardless of initial conditions.

The author suggests, therefore, the following. If neither transition programs as such nor initial conditions before the start of transition seem to have influenced the drastic fall of output decisively, then the cause(s) of a very large fall of output must be rooted elsewhere. That is, in the workings (or the mechanics) of the communist economic system. Such is, by the way, the position taken consistently by this author in his earlier writings and elaborated over time (Winiecki, 1990, 1991b, 1993, 1995).

Therefore, my proposal is to look first, in an orderly manner, at the structure of incentives in a communist centrally planned economy (whether reformed or not). This should help us to discover what types of output would be prime candidates for disappearance, or at least marked shrinkage, in the context of systemic change.

Next, the author will look for some quantitative differences in output patterns between communist planned and capitalist market economies, and then at the discernible shifts from the former to the latter, during the transition process. Having established the credentials of the determinants offered in explanation of drastic output fall, I would like to compare, in the subsequent sections, how well the theoretical explanation offered fares *vis-à-vis* other contending explanations, both in terms of internal consistency and available evidence. The chapter ends with a summary.

Structure of incentives in the communist economies and resultant distortionary output patterns

The basic hypothesis of this author has long been (see, e.g., Winiecki, 1986 and 1988) that certain system-specific characteristics induced state enterprises to report a very peculiar type of output. It was output that could only be created – in real life or in statistical reports – in the communist centrally planned economy, and nowhere else.

The fundamental consequence thereof within the framework of transition has been the existence of output that would, in consequence, disappear in an economic system that does not generate communist system-specific distortions. Since the disappearance of such output would be associated with the change in the structure of incentives, both formal and informal, I suggest to start with an analysis of the incentives in the communist economic system that generated such output in the first place.

As these incentives generated a wide range of distortionary output patterns, let me present the more important ones, beginning with what I dubbed years ago as "measurement without markets" (Winiecki, 1991: 32). There is a high cost of measuring economic performance in the case of complex goods and activities. The necessary reliance on measurement by proxy may give rise to moral hazard, as stressed by the property rights' school. Where performance is too costly to be measured in its entirety, measurement is limited to a few variables only. Economic agents are then tempted to concentrate on these few variables and neglect the performance along with other variables (see, North, 1990). This moral hazard was strongly amplified in communist economies by the lack of markets and inefficient property rights structure (on the comparative analysis of the latter, see Pejovich, 1990, and Winiecki, 1992). In a nutshell, when managers and workers are paid by what they *tell* (i.e. report to higher authorities) rather than by what they *sell*, incentives are created to doctor the reports to one's pecuniary advantage. The whole range of manipulative techniques emerged in due time in the communist economies.

The first, and the simplest, way of doctoring reports was limited to reporting higher output than was actually the case. Given the measurement costs without markets that verify, through sales transactions, the validity of the claims, such claims stood a reasonable chance of not being discovered by those on the higher rungs of the economic bureaucracy. Russians gave such doctoring the appropriate name *pripiski* (write-ins).

The second set of manipulative techniques concerned hidden changes in output structure. Thus, first, enterprises made changes in the output mix, by increasing the weight of higher-priced substitutes. Increased aggregate output value enabled managers and workers to fulfill or exceed plan target more easily. Second, enterprises made adverse changes in output quality, using substandard inputs without corresponding downward price changes. Using lower-priced inputs enabled enterprises to record higher profits and (if substandard inputs were more easily available) also higher output quantities. And, third, enterprises introduced *pseudo*-innovations, that is products whose price increases, relative to prices of standard goods, were disproportionately high in comparison with minor improvements in output characteristics. This time, managers and workers enjoyed the benefits of exceeding output value targets through sharp upward price adjustments.

In all the foregoing manipulations no extra output had, in fact, been produced. The only outcome of all these output value manipulations was hidden, i.e. unmeasured, inflation (there is a wide body of literature on hidden inflation, referred, *inter alia*, in Winiecki, 1988, Ch.2).

The major problem with the incentives in the communist economic system was that they were positively correlated with the volume or value of output, but were not negatively correlated with the cost of production (see, i.a., Grossman, 1963, and Winiecki, 1982). This stemmed from a combination of quantity/value output orientation of incentives (disregarding efficiency, quality, etc.) and the lack of responsibility for financial failure (called by Kornai, 1979, "soft" budget constraint) at the enterprise level. Thus, it paid enterprises to maximize, rather than minimize, input/output ratios. High-cost production was valued by enterprises more than low-cost production.

Where costs do not matter, inputs are in high demand, and they were in the system in question. Such "soft" budget constraint generated excess demand, unsatisfied (and unsatisfiable!) excess demand generated shortages, shortages aggravated supply uncertainty and – in order to insure themselves against late or missing deliveries – enterprises tried to hold as large input inventories as possible (see the mechanism described in Kornai, 1986, and Winiecki, 1988).

A special, even more costly system-specific output was produced, wherever enterprises – threatened by the same uncertainty of supply – decided to produce some inputs in-house rather than to rely on outside suppliers. As unspecialized, often small-scale, producers they did not benefit from the learning curve effect, to say nothing about possible scale economies. As a result, the cost *per* unit was usually higher than in specialized firms producing such product, sometimes exorbitantly so. The more sophisticated the product, the larger was the cost differential. Quite clearly, whether as inputs used in current production or as input inventories, such output was the product of the particular structure of incentives and should be expected to disappear with the change in incentives.

Not only were inventories in high demand where cost did not matter and there was no penalty for financial failure, but so too was investment. Investment demand was all the more understandable, as persistent shortages prodded central planners to do something about it. Since they were unable (or unwilling, see Winiecki (1991)) to change the structure of incentives, they tried to alleviate shortages through increased production and that meant more investment. Even more than in the case of current output, central planners were unable to measure either the rationale or costs of future investment.

Enterprises enjoyed informational advantage over their superiors and usually had the upper hand in these interactions. In consequence, not only there was too much investment, because it required less effort in an enterprise to have another production line than to increase productivity, but also a large part of that investment was extremely inefficiently used.

General purpose machinery (such as, e.g., lathes) was used only occasionally, wherever, say, an installed machine broke down and certain parts had to be produced in-house in the user enterprise because it took less time to do so than to wait for the service team from the negligent producer. Trucks were used occasionally, wherever deliveries were late and managers wanted to speed up the process. Buses were used twice a day only, in order to bring in labor from distant places to ensure that they did not turn to another state enterprise (as labor was also in short supply), and so on. Such non-core investment was, just like persistent input shortages, system-specific.

The author would like to stress that the foregoing survey showed only the most important types of output dependent on the existence of a particular structure of incentives. Their importance has been derived from their share in the registered aggregate output in communist economies. Other examples of distortionary output exist aplenty, such as excess transportation resulting from the combination of the vertical subordination of enterprises and supply uncertainty that forced the pattern of supply from "own" enterprises, regardless of how far they were located from the place where a given input was used.

Empirical evidence of system-specific output expected to disappear in transition

It is, no doubt, a demanding task to measure the size of "output that was not," or in Besançon's (1984) term the size of a "phantom economy." However, the recalculation of both official output levels and output growth rates of the former Soviet Union was a quite frequently undertaken analytical task, sometimes on the recurrent basis (such as, e.g., periodic CIA estimates of the Soviet output). Such efforts were also often undertaken at the micro level by analysts in communist countries themselves, however without the (rather dangerous) attempts to generalize on various manipulative practices to aggregate output level and growth rates. It is only in the last decade of communism, the 1980s, when such daring attempts took place.

The largest volume of recalculated statistics concerned the communist bastion, the Soviet Union. Table 1.2 presents four different time series:

- Soviet official GDP (or more precisely NMP, i.e. net material product, Soviet style GDP) growth rates;
- American recalculations done by CIA;
- Results of the comparative study of the UN Economic Commission for Europe, using comparable physical output indicators;
- Results of the academic Russian study using similar, although more detailed, physical output methodology.

Stripped of most manipulative practices, closer-to-actual growth rates turned out to be markedly, sometimes even drastically lower. American estimates revealed that more realistically calculated Soviet growth rates amounted to about 2/3 of the officially registered ones. The UN study showed registered rates to be somewhat less than that, while the Russian academic study estimated actual Soviet growth to be even more drastically lower. Although

Table 1.2 Official Soviet statistics and various unofficial estimates of annual economic growth rates in the USSR, 1951–1985

Period	Soviet official	CIA	ECE United Nations	Russian unofficial
1951–55	. . .	7.6	5.1	. . .
1956–60	. . .	7.1	5.2	. . .
1961–65	10.2	. . .	. . .	7.2
1966–70	6.5	5.1	5.4	4.4
1971–75	5.7	3.7	3.9[a]	3.2
1976–80	4.2	2.6[b]	. . .	1.0
1981–85	3.5	. . .[b]	. . .	0.6

Sources: Soviet official statistics; various US Congress materials supplied by CIA; European Commission for Europe Bulletin, 1980; and Khanin, 1988.

Notes
a   1971–73 only.
b   Alternative CIA estimates were 2.3 percent *per annum* in 1976–80 and 1.9 percent in 1981–85.

the extent of downward adjustment differed from one five-year period to another, overall the realistic output growth rate amounted to about half of the official rate, with a tendency for the non-existent part of output to increase its share over time as communist economies moved from the slowdown to decline. Clearly, declining *real* performance generated more doctoring of statistics at all levels (contrary to assertions of, e.g., Nove, who insisted on the existence of a "law of equal cheating" that made figures for various period comparable over time).

Was the Soviet Union unique in this respect? Certainly not! The comparative UN study estimated growth rates (and absolute levels) for other European communist countries as well. It showed that more realistic, physical indicator-based growth rates, for example, for the former GDR and Romania tended to deviate downward from the official rates even more than was the case for the Soviet Union.

And it should be noted that these were calculations for the period 1950–73, not including the more recent period of aggravating problems in communist economies. Informally, a Polish econometrician took the alleged Romania's GNP *per capita* in the 1980s as a starting point and then ran its official growth rates backwards. The effect was that by late 1950s Romania's GNP *per capita* approached zero. Various estimates showed that East German official figures were no less inflated than Romania's, although from a higher absolute level. Other communist countries of the region were not paragons of virtue, either, but the extent of distortions was usually smaller.

Summing up, "output that was not" was for decades a large component, often more than half of the officially registered growth rate. Other variables were no less distorted upwards. The foregoing not only affected GNP *per capita* level that was actually achieved in communist countries – in contrast with the levels calculated officially – but also implied that, in the case of a shift from the communist centrally planned to capitalist market economy, growth rates would decline for that reason alone. Quite obviously, output that existed only in official statistics would unavoidably disappear therefrom, as official statistics were the only place it could be found.

The story of "output that was, but should not" (under any less distortionary conditions) was more complicated, but also verifiable empirically to some extent. A large – in fact the largest – part of the otherwise unneeded output consisted of oversized inventories. I stressed already in the preceding section that supply uncertainty generated excessive inventories. Of course, from the viewpoint of enterprises, as stressed eloquently by Kornai (1986), inventories are never excessive. They were simply a near-costless insurance against stoppages due the lack of inputs (near-costless due to "soft" budget constraint).

As a result, the aggregate inventories-to-output ratio was throughout the whole existence of communist planned economies 2 to 2.5 times higher than

Table 1.3 The aggregate inventories-to-GDP ratio in selected communist
economies (estimates in percent)

Country		Share
Czechoslovakia	1977	70.6%
	1984	72.6%
Hungary	1982	81.0%
	1988	69.0%
Poland	1973	57.8%[a]
	1985	51.4%[a]
USSR	1985	79.0%
Memorandum item:		
United States	mid-1980s	(30.0–33.0%)

Sources: Estimates based on national statistical yearbooks; for USSR, corrected estimates from
Shmelev and Popov, 1989.

Note
a Without animal stock in agriculture.

in mature capitalist market economies. Table 1.3 shows the calculations of
the foregoing ratio in selected communist economies, fluctuating roughly
between 60 percent and 80 percent of the estimated GDP; for comparison, the
same ratio in the USA in the mid-1980s fluctuated only between 30 percent
and 33 percent.

In actual fact, these wasteful disproportions were even larger. Table 1.4
gives us the internal ratio between input inventories and output inventories.
The differences are striking. In market economies the ratio in question
fluctuated around 1:1, while in communist economies input inventories
exceeded output inventories 3:1 to 6:1. Such waste simply could not survive
intact the systemic change.

It is not only in industry that the structure of incentives generated an
enormous amount of waste in the sense of the otherwise unneeded output.
These unneeded goods had to be transported somewhere. Moreover, they had
to be transported under a distorted structure of incentives resulting from the
so-called vertical subordination of enterprises. In the general climate of
shortages the probability of delivery increased, whenever a supplying firm
was administratively subordinated to the same ministry as the supplied firm.
A threat of a cut in reward for the management of the former in case of late
or non-delivery was more credible if issued under the same administrative
umbrella. Major (1983) calculated that $1 of the GDP required three to five
times higher transport intensity (measured in freight ton/kilometers) in
communist planned than in capitalist market economies. Figure 1.3 presents
the patterns in terms of transport intensity changes over time (or changing

Table 1.4 Input inventories-to-output ratio in manufacturing industries in selected communist and capitalist economies in 1981–1985

Country	Ratio
Communist planned economies	
Bulgaria	5.07
Czechoslovakia	3.07
Hungary	6.10
Poland	4.49
Soviet Union	3.16
Capitalist market economies	
Austria	1.06
Germany	0.71
Japan	1.09
Portugal	1.66
Sweden	0.81
United Kingdom	1.02
United States	1.02

Source: Kornai (1992a).

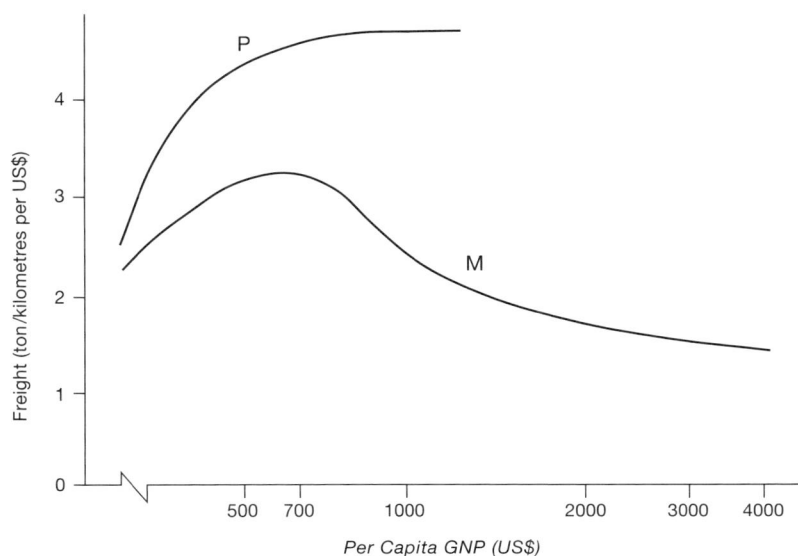

Figure 1.3 Transport intensity in some communist centrally planned and capitalist market economies over time and across GNP per capita spectrum.

Source: Major, 1983.

GNP *per capita* levels). Again, change in the structure of incentives must generate the change in the patterns of demand for transport services.

In terms of the amount of waste, the excess demand for and excessively high growth rates of investment, or capital expenditures, come close second to the excessive inventories. As shown already by Pryor (1985) for three decades the ratio of gross fixed capital investment to GDP was almost twice as high as in market economies. In other words, Table 1.5 shows that to achieve 1 percent growth of GDP communist economies needed 2 percent growth of capital expenditures, while market economies needed only 1 percent growth. This wasteful contrast was noted occasionally by some Sovietologists (see, e.g., Sirc, 1981). The systemic change-related comment is the same here as in earlier cases.

What should have been expected to happen and what did happen in early transition

The systemic change from communist centrally planned to capitalist market economy must have brought about important changes in the level and structure of economic activity. The distortions described and evidenced earlier in the communist economies were expected to disappear (sooner or later). The speed of adjustment depended on the perception by the dominant class of economic agents (that is state enterprises) concerning the inevitability and irreversibility of change – and, therefore, the inevitability of adjustment to the new "rules of the game."

We should note in passing here that a small but – predictably – fast-growing class of new private economic agents did not carry a backlog of input inventories. They would play the market game treating the new incentive

Table 1.5 Gross fixed capital investment-to-GDP: ratio of respective growth rates during a 30-year period (1950–1979) in selected communist and capitalist economies

Communist economies	Ratio	Capitalist economies	Ratio
Bulgaria	2.04	Canada	0.95
Czechoslovakia	1.66	Finland	1.01
East Germany	2.26	Greece	1.15
Hungary	2.43	Italy	0.97
Poland	2.35	Netherlands	1.11
Romania	1.95	Sweden	1.13
Soviet Union	1.62	Germany (FRG)	1.17
Average (unweighted)	2.04	Average (unweighted)	1.07

Source: Pryor, 1985.

structure as something normal, not requiring specific adjustments. We deal with the new private economic agents in th next chapter.

For the old state sector firms, output changes were influenced by the nature of distortions themselves, whose disappearance might have required more or less time for correction. Some distortions would disappear almost overnight. With the changed structure of incentives, the doctoring of reported output numbers would not offer any advantages since any enterprise could sell only what it produced (not what it reported to the respective statistical office). Under the new structure of incentives there would, then, be no *pripiski* any more.

It would also begin to matter how good the products were and what assortment of goods or services a firm offered. Therefore, other manipulative practices, if tried, would be very quickly abandoned under the threat of losing the firm's customers. The lowering of input quality, while maintaining the same price, would also survive no more than a few months. The same would happen in the case of supplying an allegedly innovative product at a higher price; it would simply not survive the market test. And, finally, trying to sell higher-priced versions, where demand is mostly for the lower-priced ones, would quickly generated excessive output inventories, weakening the firm's financial health. All that would shave off between one-third and two-thirds of the output growth rate reported in the communist past.

More typical for communist economies excessive *input* inventories would be strongly affected by systemic change. A part of systemic change is the "hardening" of a notoriously "soft" budget constraint. The Damocles' sword of financial failure, that is bankruptcy, would discipline the enterprise management. The consequences thereof were felt strongly in the area of inventories.

State enterprises willy-nilly had to adjust and they decided to significantly cut new orders for inputs, given the existence of very high inventories. Running down inventories rather than ordering new inputs made sense in more ways than one. It freed a part of the financial resources, frozen in excessive inventories (unneeded under the new conditions of market discipline) and, moreover, allowed firms to earn windfall profits by using inputs obtained at low, controlled prices and selling their final output at high, liberalized prices. There should be, then, no surprise that the beginning of transition was characterized by a sharp inventory liquidation process. It was most marked in those countries where elites were widely perceived to be serious about the systemic change and, consequently, imparted the necessary dose of credibility to the respective transition programs.

The rate of decrease of inventories has been very high in the three countries for which calculations have been made. In the 1989–92 period the level of aggregate inventories decreased in real terms in the Czech Republic by 43.7

percent, in Hungary by 41.1 percent, and in Poland by 65 percent. Precise calculation of inventories is particularly difficult in conditions of high and variable inflation; the higher and more variable it is, the less precise the calculation. Therefore, calculations for Poland in particular should be treated with caution, as Poland went through a period of near-hyperinflation.

However, even if the results for Poland may look exaggerated, the 50 percent decline – also very large – might be acceptable as Poland started its transition earlier than the Czech Republic by a year and earlier than Hungary by about half a year. The estimates are shown in Table 1.6. Clearly, current output had to decline significantly as a result of sharply cut orders for new inputs.

Another type of empirical evidence is offered by aggregate inventory-to-GDP ratio, which declined in the Czech Republic from 0.941 to 0.593 by the end of 1992 (Kouba, 1993). The latter number suggests a fall in inventories, relative to (the also falling) output by an equivalent of about 35 percent of the then Czech GDP. Even if these numbers may look exaggerated (as the output numbers are most probably referring to net material product rather than gross domestic product, which is larger), the direction and large size of the fall correlates strongly with the earlier figures.

In fact, the inventory adjustment has been larger than suggested by the numbers above since it was associated with another process of making post-communist economies more like normal, capitalist market economies. Namely, the ratio between input and output inventories began to change as well. The respective ratios of input inventories-to-output inventories in industry from Table 1.4 changed accordingly:

* in Hungary from 6.10 to 1.76 ; and
* in Poland from 4.49 to 2.32;

both by the end of 1993.

Table 1.6 Change in aggregate inventories in real terms in some post-communist economies in the early transition period, 1989–1992 (estimates in percent)[a]

Post-communist economy	1992 level (1989 level = 100%)
Czech Republic	56.3%
Hungary	58.9%
Poland	35.0%

Sources: Calculations based on national statistical yearbooks.

Note
a Aggregate inventories at current prices deflated by producer prices in industry.

Changes in the aggregate inventories-to-GDP and input inventories-to-output inventories ratios did not put post-communist transition leaders in the same class as mature, capitalist market economies. The fall, already mentioned, in aggregate inventories-to-GDP ratio at 59.3 percent of GDP still left the Czechs with almost twice as high a ratio as that of the United States.

The differential is explainable by two determinants. The first is that the ratio would continuously decline, although after the initial sharp cut, it might decline more slowly. The second is that the ratios depend not only on the structure of incentives, deformed as it was in communist economies, but also on the level of economic development. The lower the level the higher the ratios. Since post-communist countries largely belong to the class of middle-developed economies, they display (albeit decreasingly) somewhat higher ratios than mature Western economies. Note that in Table 1.4 the one country with the input inventories-to-output inventories ratio significantly above 1:1, that is 1.66:1 (still somewhat lower than in communist economies), is Portugal, the only middle-developed Western economy in that table.

Incidentally, output fall might have been higher for reasons less well understood even by those who followed closely communist economies. The discipline of the market that forced state enterprises for the first time to search for customers also entailed readjustment of output structure to suit the demand structure. That, however, meant also less output in value terms.

To explain the above let me refer to my earlier article (Winiecki, 1991), where I stressed that in transition steel mills, rather than producing as few sizes and grades of steel products as in the communist past, would have to enlarge the product variety in order to increase the salability of their products. But the increase in variety of offered inputs meant *lower* output value. Say 10,000 thicker steel sheets were priced more (given the cost of material) than 10,000 thinner sheets, always desired by customers, but unavailable earlier because the structure of incentives made it profitable to produce thicker plates only. Thus, not only inventories fell sharply, but also salable output declined in value.

Given the persistent excess demand of state enterprises for investment, its decline should have been expected with the same near-certainty as decline in inventories. There are, however, certain variations on the theme. In the case of investment, it was stressed strongly (and supported empirically) that communist economies invested more per unit of GDP than market economies. At the same time, specialists in the field knew very well that the same state firms, due to their technological obsolescence, were in dire need of investment to upgrade their capital stock.

Thus, what should have been expected to happen were parallel developments. Aggregate investment would first fall, reflecting new caution on the part of the dominant state enterprises affected by hardening budget constraint, and then recover to accompany the badly needed restructuring in old state (or already privatized) firms and the emergence of the new private firms in successfully transforming economies. In *un*successfuly transforming economies investment would be erratic or stagnating at low levels. And this is what largely happened in East-Central Europe as evidenced by Table 1.7.

Moreover, there would be, *inter alia*, a structural change within the machinery and equipment part of aggregate investment expenditures. That is core investment, upgrading the machinery and equipment used in main production lines, would increase, while non-core investment in ancillary activities typical of communist "shortage economies" (see Kornai, 1980), would shrink considerably.

There is little direct evidence of the latter, but the indirect evidence of fast-increasing productivity in industry and elsewhere is easily available. It suggests that – in contrast with the communist past – investment is made nowadays where it brings measurable productivity effects, rather than where it increases reliability of functioning of state firms, because reliability has been ensured by the structure of incentives in transition economies.

A certain type of excess demand had disappeared forever, such as demand for general purpose metal-working machinery, trucks, buses, etc., demanded under the communist economic system by every enterprise to alleviate the supply uncertainty. Thus, the historical process of specialization, interrupted

Table 1.7 Gross fixed capital investment in East-Central European economies in 1989–1998 (1989 = 100 percent)

Country	1992	1994	1998
Bulgaria	62.3%	51.9%	42.1%
Czech Republic	87.7%	94.9%	114.3%
Hungary	81.1%	93.0%	115.0%
Poland	87.7%	95.8%	186.1%
Romania	48.9%	64.0%	58.1%
Slovakia[a]	72.1%	69.9%	134.9%
Memorandum item:			
Slovenia	73.5%	92.8%	148.7%

Source: Calculated from *Countries in Transition*, 1999, the Vienna Institute for International Economic Studies (WIIW), Vienna.

Note

a   For the lack of data the fall in 1990 *vis-à-vis* 1989 was taken to be that for the Czech Republic (–2.2 percent).

by communism, has been restarted, and by both sets of economic agents: restructuring old state firms (or recently privatized ones) and by new private firms.

The end of the vertically administered communist economy should bring also about the sharp fall in demand for transportation services. And the demand for them should be expected to shrink more than for industrial output. The rationale of such expectations is derived from what has been written on pp. 20–22. Not only there would be less to transport (as unneeded, communist system-specific output disappeared from the transition economies), but also vertical subordination of enterprises to various ministries would be abolished. The latter measure would, then, end the aberrations of transporting inputs over hundreds of kilometers from distant but "own" (that is subordinated) suppliers, raising the cost of heavy and bulky, but low-priced, inputs. And this fall in transport services in excess of the well-documented fall in industrial output is what happened everywhere.

Next, among the major contributors to a very large output fall in early transition has been a non-economic factor, not considered earlier here. I stressed, however, elsewhere (see, *inter alia*, Winiecki, 1993 and 1995) that political transition from communism to democracy also entails a shift away from aggressive military strategy and, consequently, the reduction in orders for military hardware.

Finally, it is worth noting that almost all the distortions generated by the communist system, whose correction should have been expected with the collapse of communist economy, have most adversely affected industry. All these numerous corrections would necessarily affect the scale of the fall of industrial output. Thus, e.g., all post-communist economies registered a larger fall of industrial output than of GDP in the first years of transition. Another measure of the same phenomenon has been the fall in the *share* of industry in post-communist economies in transition (see Table 1.8), indicating a disproportionately larger correction of past distortions in industry than in the remaining sectors.

Dissolution of COMECON: real cause or red herring in the debate?

A majority of analysts taking part in the debate on the causes of output fall tended to single out the dissolution of COMECON, the communist quasi-integrative grouping, as yet another – maybe even the most important – source of the very large fall in output. These analysts hardly asked what in my opinion is the most pertinent question: was demand for goods from other communist countries in any way different from demand for goods from their domestic, also communist, economy? Or, to put it more precisely, were

Table 1.8 Changing shares of industrial sector in GDP in East-Central European economies in 1990–1998 (in percentages)

Country	1990	1992	1994	1998
Bulgaria	50.0%	43.2%	36.5%	25.5%
Czech Republic	46.4%	43.5%	39.3%	37.6%
Hungary	30.9%	29.6%	27.6%[a]	29.0%
Poland	41.8%	41.6%	38.6%[a]	32.8%
Romania	45.9%	40.0%	40.7%[a]	40.8%
Slovakia	. . .	38.0%	38.7%[a]	31.6%
Memorandum item:				
Slovenia	38.7%	37.6%	35.1%	33.1%

Sources: *Countries in Transition*, 1995 and 1999, the Vienna Institute for International Economic Studies (WIIW), Vienna.

Note
a 1993.

incentives generating that demand different from those operating in the domestic economy? It is answers to the foregoing questions that offer clues as to why intra-COMECON trade should have been expected to fall dramatically, in line with the domestic demand in early transition.

In what follows this author draws heavily on his article (see Winiecki, 2000a). For reasons difficult to understand, the end of the institutional arrangement that maintained COMECON has been regarded as the major source of trade decline among its ex-members. Some analysts simply – but as we shall see erroneously – ascribed trade and, consequently, output losses to the dissolution of that institution (e.g. Fischer and Gelb, 1991). Others went even further, blaming post-communist countries in transition for their unwillingness to band together to "soften the blow," whatever that might mean. In the opinion of many the deliberate decision of East-Central European policy-makers to end the "COMECON story" entailed a considerable cost to their societies, with a dramatic fall in intra-regional trade.

Rare were assessments such as those of Kornai (1994) or Aslund (1994) who stressed rightly that COMECON trade patterns were dependent on the fundamental features of the communist economic system and, with the disappearance of that system, trade links would be strongly affected as well. Since changes in the structure of production were unavoidable in transition, as explained and evidenced so far, changes in foreign trade were inevitably to follow.

To answer the fundamental question posed at the beginning of this section, sources of the steep decline in trade among former members of COMECON are generally the same as general sources of output. Note that it is only the trade in raw materials that (largely) survived the end of communism because it was based on near-world market prices for corresponding quality. However, most of the trade consisted of intermediate inputs and investment goods, usually of substandard quality and saleable on the COMECON markets only due to the generalized excess demand and "soft" budget constraint. Another component was, no less substandard, consumer goods (saleable due to the same shortages).

Once countries entered the path of transition, demand for an overwhelming part of these imports disappeared for the same reasons that demand for domestically produced inputs and investment goods fell sharply. With the "hardening" of budget constraint state firms cut down input orders and eliminated unnecessary investments. Furthermore, the remaining orders were often placed where it was more profitable and not where state firms were earlier ordered to place them.

One extra determinant of the rapid fall of demand for imports from ex-COMECON countries should also be brought into the picture. It is the near-simultaneity of transition, at least of the East-Central European countries. Poland, Hungary, former Czechoslovakia, and, more haphazardly, Bulgaria and Romania all started stabilization *cum* liberalization programs within one year's time span. Thus, the behavior of, say, Polish firms affected not only domestic production but also production in other ex-COMECON countries as orders for, primarily, unneeded inputs or unneeded investment goods imported from, say, Hungary or Czechoslovakia were cut severely or cancelled altogether. And, since about every country in the region, except for the former Soviet Union, started at about the same time, producers felt the simultaneous impact of sharply reduced system-specific demand both at home and in other transition countries. Since a very large part of intra-COMECON trade was of the sort described here, the trade with other countries of the region plummeted.

To sum up the foregoing, there was no "willful abandonment" of the trade with other post-communist economies. Simply, with the launching of a decentralized market system, microeconomic decisions of state and privatized firms corrected the distortions inherited from the communist economic system and eliminated demand for goods unneeded under normal circumstances, that is where prices and quality matter. The "lost" Eastern markets that could, allegedly, soften the aggregate output fall were a myth.

The foregoing considerations should make it clear that COMECON trade contribution was not in any way a "stand alone" cause of output fall, but part and parcel of the process of correcting communist system-specific distortions. And, since distortions have been system-specific, their causes have been exactly the same as the causes of distortions in the domestic economies. Therefore, the pattern of output fall must have been the same.

The range of views on determinants of early drastic output fall

The range of views expressed on the very steep fall of output in early transition has been surprisingly wide, given the already accumulated knowledge of the distortions in the communist centrally planned economies. Their protagonists looked to the variety of factors, to initial conditions at the start of transition, to macroeconomic conditions in the early period, etc. Some authors suggested a number of determinants, not necessarily consistent with each other.

There have been views intellectually close to the one elaborated earlier in this article. They differed from this one in the degree of specificity, being mostly rather general, but pointed in the direction elaborated in this article. Thus, for example, in early 1990 Sirc criticized those who complained that production had fallen or would fall after the start of transition.

> Certainly, it would fall and it *should* [emphasis added: J.W.] fall. Communist economies, on the whole, produce goods, valued at about 10 percent of the [GDP equivalent: J.W.], that go straight into inventories never to reappear because either they are of such bad quality or so expensive that nobody wants them. Another 10 percent . . . are duly installed as part of productive capacity but never used because the new capacity does not produce anything anybody wants.

> (Sirc, 1990: 5)

The reinsurance factor resulting from the general climate of uncertainty and shortage is missing from the above explanation, and quality *cum* cost factor is given prominence there. However, the author in question points toward two major contributing factors of output fall in transition, an unavoidable and desirable correction of excessive inventories and excessive investment under the communist economic system.

Siebert (1991a) stressed the same in a statement that "some of the goods produced . . . (notably many investment goods) had no positive economic value; unless generous subsidies were paid to maintain this absurdity, the switch to a market economy would give rise to welfare enhancing cuts" (p. 28). Cassel (1992) and Aslund (1994) wrote basically the same. Probably the best catchphrase for the kind of system-specific output, not demanded under more normal systemic conditions, is Balcerowicz's (1995) "pure socialist production." Some, not very many, underlined the disappearance of non-existent output that in each case subtracted a substantial share of earlier registered annual output rate (see, however, Aslund, 1994; Bratkowski, 1993; Siebert 1991b). This was the case in spite of the fact that doctored output reports had been the staple of Sovietological literature.

Taken altogether, the writings of the foregoing authors (including the author) could be classified as neo-institutional ones, stressing the legacy of the past institutional framework, including the structure of property rights and incentives, and the impact of their change on the level and structure of output in the transition process. A large dose of Schumpeterian/Hayekian thinking along the lines of natural selection/creative destruction has been present there as well.

Generally, however, those pointing to the really important factors contributing to the very large fall of output have been islands in the large sea of those writing on transition. Probably the most numerous have been those which underline the impact of the variously – and often vaguely – defined "structural factors."

Gomulka (1991, 1994, 1998) and Kornai (1993, 1994), Blanchard (1997), Cassel (1992), and Williamson (1995), to name just a few of the more prominent protagonists, formulated the foregoing views. Kornai and Cassel present some elements of their views similar to those of the author. The main thrust of their explanations lies, however, elsewhere, and combines some neo-classical and neo-institutional considerations.

They present in detail (Gomulka, 1998; Kornai, 1994; Blanchard, 1997) the output effect of what they call "internal and external liberalization." In their view, both liberalizations cause shifts in relative prices, sharp reduction of subsidies, and, in consequence, fall in demand for earlier subsidized goods. This is what some of them call "structural supply shock."

The foregoing is certainly true, but it is only half of the story. The other half is an answer to the question of where all the money went, that is on which goods financial resources of firms and households were spent instead. The above argument explains the reallocation of output, i.e., change in output structure, rather than output fall. That is, some output fall might have taken place on that account. But compared to the size of output fall due to the, for example, downward correction of inventories it has been small beer.

Raiser (1992) rightly noted that in order to maintain the structural (reallocational) causes of output fall one should prove empirically that the pattern of output fall has been industry- or branch-specific, and he posited that they were not. Clearly, he had in mind very early near-uniform output fall in the manufacturing sector of Poland, Hungary, and the Czech Republic. However, the knowledge of the past, system-specific demand distortions and the evidence collected since 1992 are able to explain *both* early near-uniformity and later differentiation in output patterns.

Output, especially industrial output, indeed fell to a similar degree in the early months of each transition. But that was, again, something that one should expect. To give an example, output in engineering and food industry fell together because excessive demand characterized both firms and households in the communist economies. Both enterprises and households held excessive inventories, enterprises of inputs for further processing and households of food products bought in excess of current consumption. Hoarding of food, part of which later rotted in households' refrigerators, was the result of the same supply uncertainty.

Once systemic change liberalized prices and the supply uncertainty was removed, households discontinued hoarding and limited their purchases to what they really needed for current consumption. An important side-effect thereof has been that the fall in registered food consumption did not necessarily mean *actual* fall.

The same story applied to investment. Excess demand was ubiquitous, and was not confined to heavy industry. Expected "harder" budget constraint after the start of transition, once again, affected investment demand across the whole economy.

Nonetheless in the short-to-medium run, say, by mid-1990 it became clearly visible that structural reallocation of demand – and, in consequence, resources – had indeed been taking place. First, as shown in Table 1.8, there was a reallocation of demand from industrial goods to services; the share of the former decreased and that of the latter increased. Second, intra-industry change had been simultaneously taking place. The range of the output fall was extremely wide: from –50.5 percent to –10.4 percent in Hungary and from –43.3 percent to –7.7 percent in Poland, for example. In both cases the largest fall was registered by basic metals. Other heavy industries also suffered strongly. But among the largest was also the fall in textiles, a light industry equivalent of "pure socialist production," as a large part of it was of very low quality and saleable only on the closed COMECON markets. Table 1.9 presents relative output changes across most manufacturing industries.

It may be added that the intra-industry, or intra-branch, changes were even larger. Kornai (1994) noted the rapid expansion of high technology output in the midst of transformational recession. Gomulka (1994) added empirical evidence from Poland: in 1989–91 changes in the output levels across 590 industrial product groups ranged from –90 percent to +50 percent and more. Thus, the reallocation of output within the framework of the aggregate fall had undoubtedly been taking place.

The problem with this very popular explanation is that it does not explain much in terms of output volume, compared with this author's explanation. For assuming that only half of the excessive inventories had been eliminated in early transition, the reduction would amount to about 10 percent GDP. This staggering demand cut would be the result of the following guesstimate. We assume that roughly half of the inventories' differential in Table 1.3 is the result of the distorted incentives; another half is the result of the differential efficiency stemming from the different levels of economic development.

Table 1.9 Changes in output levels in manufacturing industries in some East-Central European economies in 1989–1992 in percentages (1989 = 100 percent)

Industry	Czechoslovakia	Hungary	Poland
Basic metals		−50.5%[a]	−43.3%
Engineering and metal products		−47.0%[b]	−31.7%
Chemicals		−29.3%	−27.9%
Other non-metallic mineral products		−32.4%	−22.3%[d]
Wood, pulp, and paper		−15.1%	−12.2%
Textiles			−37.0%
Clothing		−45.6%[c]	−7.7%
Food and beverages		−10.4%	−28.2%

Sources: National statistical yearbooks and data files.

Notes
a Basic metals and metal products.
b Engineering products only.
c Textiles, clothing and footwear.
d Building materials only.

Since the excessive inventories in Table 1.3 amounted roughly to 40 percent GDP, the half of the half amounts to the above volume of 10 percent GDP.

An additional explanation, deemed by many to be of importance, namely that of coordination breakdown, is to me even less convincing. What Kornai (1994) calls "disruptions in coordination," Blanchard (1997) and Blanchard and Kremer (1997) call "disorganization," and Gomulka (1998) calls "knock-on effects" all amount to the same thing. These authors and many others stress the very special inter-enterprise linkages in the hierarchically organized communist economic system. Without coordination by central planners state enterprises in such conditions were supposed to be like babes in the woods, completely lost in the world of newly emerging horizontal linkages of the market.

Once the linkages with suppliers, earlier imposed from above, became based on contract, some suppliers offered their inputs elsewhere. Accordingly, final producers – it is implied – faced market demand they could not fulfill. In the reverse process, the same coordination problems affected also suppliers, as explained by Gomulka (Gomulka and Lane, 1996, and Gomulka, 1998). In his interpretation it is final goods producers who did not find demand for their goods, but not only they, but also their suppliers suffered therefrom.

Disorganization or discoordination argument is theoretically of a hybrid nature, for it comprises both supply- and demand-side components. The problem with it is that as a general thesis, pretending to explain a large part of output fall, it is simply untenable. For it assumes the existence of a sizable unsatisfied demand. However, it was a universally established phenomenon that in countries that went through the process of thorough (and therefore successful) transition unsatisfied demand very quickly evaporated. With old supply constraints removed *any* demand could be satisfied through domestic production or imports. Note however that aggregate imports did not increase in the period of the steepest output fall in early transition. They were only partly reallocated from inputs to consumer goods (see Winiecki, 2000a).

Curiously, Kornai (1994), who also subscribes to the view in question, shows in his Table 3 that in Hungary between 1988 and mid-1993 the percentage of state firms stressing insufficient demand went up from 20–25 percent to 65–69 percent. In the same Table insufficient supplies of inputs as impediments to production were mentioned by a few percent of firms only. Thus, there was little – if any – unsatisfied demand which producers of final or intermediate goods wanted to satisfy but could not, due to "disorganization" problems.

Also, what Blanchard (1997) sees as evidence of still sizable unsatisfied demand in some countries shows little more than the degree of success in transition. In the Table presented in his article, in successful countries (Czech Republic, Hungary, Poland) shortages of certain materials were noted on average by barely 5 percent of firms (similar to Kornai's evidence from Hungary), but in countries whose transition was slow, inconsistent, or derailed, it ranged from 15 percent to 25 percent. The author's conclusion is that in the latter countries there were not so much sizable pockets of unsatisfied demand, but sizable pockets of the old rules of the game, which generated behavior of firms more typical for the communist centrally planned than for capitalist market economy.

An even less convincing part of the story is the stress on disorganization in intra-COMECON trade relations. Demand for manufactured goods imported from country members of the former communist quasi-integrative grouping fell very sharply, indeed. But the reason for the fall was not because the exchanged machinery and equipment and their components (the largest part of intra-COMECON exchange) were strongly desired by all parties after the start of transition and only lack of coordination between state enterprises in the new decentralized environment prevented transactions to have been accomplished. On the contrary, they were found to be a part of "pure socialist production," that is unneeded under the new, healthier structure of incentives.

Some problems of that sort might have appeared in the countries of former Soviet Union, where systemic change, however inconsistent, overlapped with the breakdown of the state. But even there the disappearance of demand for system-specific high inventories, investment, and military goods had an overwhelmingly stronger impact.

Another popular strand, or rather strands, of thinking saw the main cause of output fall in macroeconomic policy measures, or more precisely in macroeconomic policy stance. From the very beginning of transition, complaints about too restrictive a macroeconomic policy stance had been strongly heard (see, e.g., Laski, 1990; Bhaduri and Laski, 1992; Nuti, 1992). They, and many others, stressed the restrictiveness of fiscal and monetary policies. The weakest part of that argument has already been exposed in the context of the coordination breakdown argument. There is, simply, very little, if any, empirical evidence of unsatisfied demand which could have been satisfied with a more accommodative macroeconomic policies. Most of the output that disappeared would have disappeared anyway, for the output in question was overwhelmingly unneeded under the market structure of incentives.

Besides, these views were expressed very early, when the experience was limited to countries now regarded as transition "success stories." The later experience of countries which pursued much weaker versions of transition, with much less macroeconomic restraint, as well as countries that pursued no meaningful transition at all, and yet suffered from the very large output fall, revealed the untenability of these views.

A more sophisticated version of the view looking at the macroeconomic policy as the main culprit of the output fall is the Calvo-Coricelli (Calvo and Coricelli, 1993) model of "credit crunch." With the interest rates approaching the positive level in real terms, unreformed banks refused to continue to offer revolving credit for the purchase of inputs by (presumably economically healthy) state enterprises. Or enterprises themselves refused to borrow at high interest rates and reduced output accordingly. But the "credit crunch" model cannot withstand the strength of the repeatedly mentioned absence of unsatisfied demand. This author has already quoted various survey results. Berg and Blanchard (1994) tested the "credit crunch" hypothesis on Polish data and rejected it as a generalized, i.e., economically significant, explanation.

There were other, less frequently heard, opinions on the steep output fall issue. Both the arguments already presented and those that were not suffer from the same weakness. They might have marginally influenced the output patterns, but they are simply contradicted by the evidence accumulated over the period of more than a decade.

Brief note about outliers

The inevitable, very large output fall in the phase of "transformational" recession affected – as stressed at the beginning of this chapter – both transition leaders and transition laggards. The difference was largely in the path of output, with a steeper but shorter period of output fall in successful transition countries, and a less steep, but longer-lasting, fall period in transition laggards. A much greater difference was registered in the recovery period, which was much weaker, or non-existent, in the latter countries.

Contrary to the expectations of politicians, pundits, and even the majority of academics, the different patterns of recovery (or the lack of recovery as it happened in some cases) depended rather little on the performance of the state enterprise sector. And this was true regardless of the speed of adjustment of state enterprises or privatized ex-state enterprises. The most important factor was the dynamics of the *new*, entrepreneurial private sector. This story, however, will be told in detail in Chapter 2.

What remains to be explained toward the end of this chapter is the existence of "outliers." The statistical term in question refers here to those countries whose pattern of output fall markedly differed from the rest of post-communist economies, that is Belarus and Uzbekistan, where output fall was in the early period much smaller than elsewhere.

The Belarus case is simple. Very little transition to the market had been accomplished there. And whatever little had been accomplished was partly reversed after Lukashenka's ascent to the presidency/dictatorship. As a result, many of the characteristics of the output pattern in Belarus are not much different from those of the orthodox centrally planned economy. Brazen *pripiski* continue to be present in state enterprises, including farms (both state and collective). And so are manipulations of quality, assortment, and pseudo-innovations. Not only do output reports continue to be doctored, but behavior traditional under central planning is also flourishing. Demand for investment remains high and so is the level of input inventories. Also, according to various reports, military weaponry is produced in quantities exceeding Belarus and Russia's needs (or at least payment abilities).

There is little surprise, then, that "pure socialist production" (including production which does not exist) accounts for a substantial part of output. The unneeded output would undoubtedly disappear under the conditions of any seriously pursued transition to the market, but no such systemic change is expected in the foreseeable future. A flip side of the situation is that, given such a large share of the "pure socialist production," the distance in living standards between Belarus and successful transition countries has increased sharply, in spite of the fact that output in the latter countries fell initially by much more than it did in Belarus.

Uzbekistan's case is much more interesting because it is a good example of erroneous way of thinking about post-communist transition in Europe. True, the old communist rules of the game continue to dominate in Uzbekistan's economy as well. But Uzbekistan has what may be called a "China advantage" of relative underdevelopment. This allowed it to continue with some real GDP growth in certain areas in parallel to the decline elsewhere in the economy.

Those analysts who, without much (if any) reflection, compare the marketization of the Chinese communist economy since 1978 with the radical transition (political and economic) of post-communist Europe, often come to the conclusion that the Chinese offer a path to follow for East-Central and East Europeans (see, for example, Stiglitz, 1999).

There are, however, striking differences between the *communist* reform accepting the continuing expansion of the non-state sector in China and *post-communist* political and economic transition, which makes any repetition of the Chinese path impossible (see, i.a., Csaba, 1996, and Raiser, 1995). Moreover, there is also a striking difference in the level of economic development between China – and Uzbekistan – on the one hand and European post-communist economies on the other.

Uzbekistan is much less economically developed than Russia or countries of the Western rim of the former Soviet Union (let alone the Czech Republic, Hungary, or Poland). Therefore, the unavoidable and desirable shrinkage of the state, largely heavy, industry has not affected it as much as it did the latter countries. Its agriculture, however inefficient, is a more secure base for the slow transition to the market. This is so because most of the labor shift in Uzbekistan is, as in underdeveloped China, from agriculture to light industry in accordance with the standard development pattern of the nineteenth and twentieth centuries in the non-communist world. By contrast in more developed post-communist countries there is a dramatic shedding of superfluous output (and inevitably labor) in heavy industry that, then, may shift to light industry (always a difficult process) or to services. Thus, under-developed Uzbekistan may copy to some extent the path of a still more underdeveloped China – but that is as far as any sensible copying might go.

Summary

The chapter began with a theoretical analysis of determinants of output fall in post-communist economies in transition, based on the structure of incentives characteristic for communist economies, as well as with an empirical one, showing the enormous potential for the fall in "pure socialist production" during the systemic change. Thus, a list of quantitatively most important determinants contributing to "pure socialist production," expected to disappear in transition, was drawn and the most probable impact suggested.

The conclusions were unequivocal. First, the steep output fall in early transition, or what Kornai called "transformational recession," was to be expected and its causes are easily explained by the legacy of the distorted Soviet-type, or communist, economy. And, second, it was not only expected, but also, as stressed by Sirc, desirable. For the kind of output that disappeared was the kind of output not demanded any more under the transition to the market regime.

Thus, the fall of ouput was inextricably linked to the past. Not only did transition eliminate unneeded "pure socialist production," but also output fall took place in the old enterprise sector, first and foremost in the state enterprise sector. However, the distorted world of Soviet-type economies (incidentally the title of my 1988 book) distorted the behavior of *all* economic agents, regardless of ownership. Detailed statistics for Poland reveal that cooperative sector and even the private sector were adversely affected and shrank in terms of output and employment (see Chapter 5), while analysis of early transition in Hungary (see Chapter 3) suggests similar pattern of decline. And, just as output fall was the legacy of the old, that is the communist past, so output recovery was to be associated primarily with the present, that is with the expansion of the new, overwhelmingly private sector. The story is told in the next chapter.

2 Transformational recovery and the impact of the new private sector

Jan Winiecki

Introduction

Transformational recession differs in its character from cyclical recession. Unsurprisingly, transformational recovery also differs from cyclical recovery. In transformational recession a very large fall of output results primarily from the changed structure of incentives during the systemic change that once for all eliminated demand for "pure socialist production." In transformational recovery we register, as in cyclical recovery, output increase, but by contrast there is a simultaneous major change on the supply side. For it is *new* (overwhelmingly private) firms that increasingly supply the market.

We observe also a change of focus, not noted in the traditional cyclical recovery and recession. Schumpeterian "creative destruction" is at work in the latter. In recession some firms fail, while innovators grow dynamically in spite of adverse business conditions. In recovery most firms resume growth at a slower or faster rate. But the analysis focuses by and large on firms that already existed at the start of the business cycle.

In transformational recession the focus is different. There, old firms, that is overwhelmingly state-owned firms, which existed before the beginning of transition, make the most difference. They sharply reduce output and (more slowly) employment. In transformational recovery the focus is – or, in the view of the author should be – largely on *new* firms, which did not exist before transformation, or transition, began.

The foregoing does not mean that new firms did not play any role in early transition, during the steep fall of aggregate output. However, due to the fact that they were start-up firms (apart from the not very numerous private holdovers from the communist past), their positive contribution to aggregate output was unable to balance the strongly negative contribution of old state (and privatized) firms.

At least in the successful transition economies new private firms were both fast growing in numbers and also increasing their output. However, given their small – or even non-existent – share in output, even double-digit growth rates were unable to stop the fall of output in the early transition period. Nevertheless, over time, the twofold impact of the growing number of firms and of these firms' growing output has become sufficiently large to achieve the turnaround.

By stressing the impact of new firms, or the new private sector, the author focuses on the issue largely neglected in the transition literature. It is the issue of the relative importance, or quantitatively relative weight, of the output of new, entrepreneurial private sector and the old state and privatized, i.e. ex-state, sector.

What the old state sector does in transition, at least in the short-to-medium run (three to seven years) is quite clear and well researched in the transition literature. It shrinks, faster or less fast. But the relative shares of privatized and new private sector have rarely (if at all) been studied in the economic literature on the subject.

This author posits, however, that the issue is of crucial importance for transformational recovery in post-communist economies. The internal composition of the private sector has in my opinion a strong influence on economic performance. The more thriving the new private sector, the faster its growth of output, and the larger its share in the output of the aggregate private sector (relative to the privatized sector), the better the performance of the national economy. Better performance translates itself into a shorter time of transformational recession and more robust transformational recovery (see Winiecki, 1999).

Consequently, Chapter 2 deals with various aspects of this issue. We start with considerations on the importance of the new, entrepreneurial private sector in general and in the post-communist transition in particular. Next, two "stylized facts" scenarios of transition are presented, each considering the impact of the fast-growing, thriving, and over time increasingly large new private sector. Alternatively, we consider the impact of the slow-growing, constrained, and limited private sector. Both rapid, strong recovery and slow, weak recovery are shown to be dependent primarily on the dynamism of the new private sector – or the lack of it. In the short-to-medium run net additions of privatized firms to output are small, while those to employment are non-existent.

Finally, we consider the determinants affecting the new private sector. In contrast with the traditional theorizing on transition, the author also adds to the analysis of detailed regulations and that of the transition's "Holy Trinity" (stabilization, liberalization, and privatization) a third level of analysis. It is a level of civilizational fundamentals: liberty, law and order, and trust. These play a surprisingly neglected but important role in ensuring success or failure of the systemic change.

Post-communist transition and importance of the entrepreneurial private sector

In a Voltairean manner we start with the definitions. The problem is particularly important in the empirical sense because no country statistics in post-communist countries (or elsewhere) offer much information on *de novo* private firms. At best they register newly created and recently closed firms and offer us the net balance in a given period and changes in the stock of firms over time. A major problem is that we do not know whether they are private firms (deemed to be the most dynamic – see below). There may be some newly created state firms, municipal firms, or cooperatives.

The knowledge in this respect is all the more important in post-communist economies, where the privatization process generates many spin-offs, that is separations from a very large state-owned dinosaurs of a number of independent (still state-owned) firms dealing with the activities peripheral to a normally functioning capitalist firm. An even greater problem is that the data on measurement of the new firms along various dimensions is very limited indeed.

An alternative empirical approach to the new private sector is to equate the said entrepreneurial sector with the sector of small and medium-sized firms (SMEs for short). And not without reason. Few new firms are established from the start as large ones. Therefore the population of SMEs may be, roughly, equated with that of new, entrepreneurial firms: roughly, because the SME statistics, increasingly collected on a more or less regular basis, suffer from two types of discrepancies, important from the vantage point of this study. First, as stressed already, the SME statistics do not cover the few new large firms (primarily the "green-field" foreign investment-based firms). And, second, they will cover *non*-private new small and medium-sized firms. For reasons explained in the preceding paragraphs, their numbers may be relatively large in post-communist economies undergoing a complex owner-ship transformation of state-owned firms.

There are general economic reasons for the interest in the small and medium-sized firms. In Western market economies, these firms, excluding agriculture, generate nowadays anything between 1/3 and 2/3 of GDP and between 1/2 and 3/4 of aggregate employment. Thus, they are the weighty engine of the economic activity. Table 2.1 presents the SME data on employ-ment for a majority of both large and small OECD countries, as well as for the three transition countries considered in greater details in Part II of this book (see Chapters 3–5). By the year 2000 the SMEs' share in employment in East-Central European countries in transition ranged between 60 percent and 75 percent. According to Szostkowski (2003), apart from the Czech Republic, Hungary, and Poland, the range of employment typical for Western

Table 2.1 Share of SMEs in aggregate employment in selected OECD countries
ranked from the largest to the smallest share in or near 1996 (in
percentages)

Country	Share in % of the total
Portugal	80.0
Spain	79.8
Switzerland	69.9
Denmark	68.7
Ireland	68.4
France	63.2
Netherlands	60.7
Sweden	60.3[a]
Germany	59.7
Canada	38.4[b]
USA	37.7[b]
Memorandum item:	
Hungary	70.1
Poland	63.2
Czech Republic	52.3

Sources: Calculated from OECD Small and Medium Enterprise Outlook, 2000. For Hungary:
State of Small and Medium Sized Business in Hungary, 1999.

Notes: SMEs employing up to 249 persons. Indicated separately, if calculated otherwise.

a SMEs up to 199 employees.

b SMEs up to 100 employees.

economies has been reached by Slovakia and the three Baltic countries, with
Estonia in the lead (75.2 percent of aggregate employment).

SMEs' importance reaches far beyond the economic impact upon aggregate
output and employment, even beyond their competitive advantages of
flexibility and innovative ability (the role as an agent of change, see
Acs, 2003). Seen rightly as entrepreneurial firms, with the owner-manager
overwhelmingly in charge, they are important for the social-political order,
not only for economic order. Presently about 85 percent of European
SMEs are owner-managed (see EBS, 2002). And owners-managers, i.e.
manufacturers, merchants, craftsmen, and other providers of numerous
services, have historically formed the backbone of the middle class, and the
middle class, in turn, has been the mainstay of the liberty-based order.

Moreover, they have long been perceived as upholders of hard work,
prudence, thrift, self-reliance, and other "lesser virtues" (as they were called
in Victorian times). It is upon these virtues that the capitalist market order –
and its unparalleled prosperity – has been built.

Alexis de Tocqueville noted this in his classic study, when, pointing to both entrepreneurial and civic initiatives of Americans, wrote: "What most astonished me in the United States is not so much the marvelous grandeur of some undertakings as the innumerable multitude of small ones" (*Democracy in America*, 1840).

These traditional, so to say, interests in the SME sector would suffice in themselves to justify our interest in that sector in the post-communist transition economies. But the legacy of the communist past adds several further, critically important, interests in the role of the SME sector, both non-economic and economic ones.

First, it is the entrepreneurs that are seen as important contributors to the reestablishment of the moral order, corroded or even nearly destroyed by a prolonged communist assault on the "bourgeois morality" (see, *inter alia*, Krasznai and Winiecki, 1995, and Winiecki, 1998). The capitalist market order possesses certain self-reinforcing moral properties. To give one, but important, example, traders who might have started as fly-by-night operators, often selling substandard goods from a car boot, begin to behave much more honestly once they acquire real property and settle down with their shop in a particular locality.

Neglectful about the quality of the wares they sold from a car boot, they become the most critical inspectors of goods or materials they receive from their suppliers. For they know quite well that their neglect, or plain dishonesty, will drive customers away to their competitors.

May be, in the first years, or even in the first generation, this honest behavior is perceived by many post-communist entrepreneurs as being imposed on them from the outside. But, with time, they themselves discover the famous Benjamin Franklin dictum: "Honesty is the best policy." And they will pass this wisdom to their children and heirs.

The role of reputation, with its clear economic advantages, will be increasing in post-communist economies, its speed depending on the progress of transition. It is the new private sector that will play the dominant role in that process. That applies to both domestic entrepreneurs, who on the average will be learning about the economic advantages of reputation, and foreign investors, who will mostly treat reputation as a matter of course.

Second, the new private sector is expected to contribute mightily to the emergence of the dominant private sector in the national economies of post-communist countries. Since the economic history knows no successful market economy that is based on state, or public, property, transformation countries have to reestablish structures of ownership based on the preponderance of privately owned firms. As stressed by the author (see Gruszecki and Winiecki, 1991, and Winiecki, 1992) the change in the structure of ownership in the national economy may be accomplished in two complementary ways. It is not enough to try to achieve the dominance of the private sector through the transformation of state-owned firms (SOEs) into privately owned ones, that is through what has been – and still is – erroneously called "the privatization."

Transforming SOEs into privately owned firms is only one part of the process of privatization of the national economy. That part I dubbed privatization "from above," as it entails the activism of the state in the process. A complementary, rather than alternative, way is through the establishment and expansion of the generic private sector, that is the sector of *de novo* firms. Since this way required at a minimum only enabling conditions rather than active involvement of the state, I called it privatization "from below."

In Poland, and in fact throughout the whole post-communist world, privatization "from above" dominated the public debate and policy-making to such an extent that it became for all practical purposes perceived as *the* privatization. In Chapter 5 on Poland I referred to the transition program presented by the first Polish non-communist government in October 1989. Within eight large-size newspaper pages, presenting the governmental transition program and its rationale, only **half a sentence** was devoted to the entrepreneurial sector to be established from scratch. It stressed the need to create proper competitive conditions and "full freedom in establishing new [presumably private] firms" (Program Gospodarczy, 1989: 4). All the rest dealt with what I call the "Holy Trinity" of transition: stabilization, liberalization, and privatization ("from above," of course).

Some analysts of transition, especially those who appreciate the role of privatization "from below," have been strongly critical of the foregoing bias (see, e.g., Benacek in Chapter 3 here). But this should not strike us as particularly odd when we look back to the time of the collapse of the communist system. After all, the public sector (or, as it was then called, the "socialized" sector) produced as a whole between 80 percent and 100 percent of aggregate output, as well as employing an equivalent percentage of the labor force.

Few critics knew the economics of development well enough to have paid attention to the studies by Anne Krueger (see Krueger, 1983 and 1984) and similar ones, which presented the experience of liberalizing developing countries (LDCs). In successful liberalizing LDCs ten years after the start of liberalization about half of the employment was registered in the firms that had not existed a decade earlier. The successful transition economies actually repeated the pattern in even less time. For example, between 1988 and 1994 the share of Czechoslovak industrial firms that employed fewer than 500 persons changed from 1 percent to 98.5 percent of all firms (OECD, 1996), unimaginable under normal market conditions). Almost all these firms were established since the beginning of transition in 1990.

What is striking today is that politicians, pundits, and scholars still often overlook this remarkable feature of transition. Maybe this is because for so long they tied their hope for successful radical systemic change to the transformation of state-owned enterprises. Or, as it happens sometimes, they refuse to see the phenomenon reinforcing the emerging of the capitalist market order they dislike (as, e.g, in McIntyre and Dallago (eds), 2003).

In differing proportions across the spectrum of transition countries, privatization, both "from above" and "from below," contributed to the emergence of the preponderant private sector, at least in the "success stories" of transition. Figure 2.1 gives an idea about the aggregate share of the private sector in GDP in 1999 in the national economies of transition countries.

For successful transition countries it exceeded 60 percent of the total everywhere, with Hungary and the Czech Republic approaching 80 percent. An exception among success stories was Slovenia, with its share of the private sector only approaching 55 percent. It should be noted that among countries with a high share of the aggregate private sector were a number of countries less successful in transition such as Albania, Russia, Romania, Bulgaria, etc. Clearly, the high aggregate share of the private sector, although necessary for successful transition, has not been a sufficient factor in determining the outcome of the transition process.

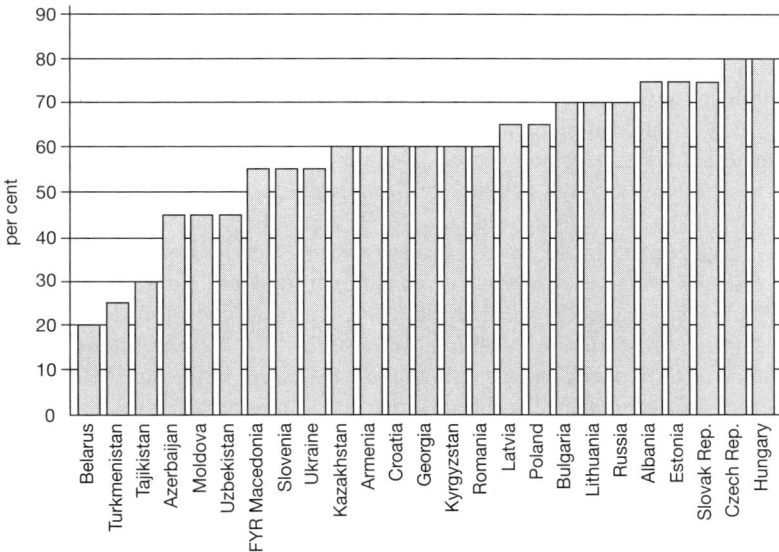

Figure 2.1 Aggregate private sector shares.
Source: Transition Report 2000, EBRD.

Third, it was not only the ownership structure, but also the size structure of the capitalist marker economy that had to be reestablished during the transition process. The distorted size structure, one of the many harmful legacies of the communist past, was heavily skewed in favor of large and very large firms. It had to undergo a radical change in order to reestablish a normally functioning network of small, middle-sized, and large firms cooperating with each other as suppliers and users of supplied goods and services. For SMEs have historically been not only producers of and traders in final goods, but also suppliers of inputs to large firms. Given their flexibility and entrepreneurial initiative, they are much more efficient in these roles than large firms would have ever been.

Table 2.2 presents the share of SMEs in aggregate output in manufacturing in selected Western countries and in the three transition countries presented in Part II of this book. Clearly, the latter largely reestablished the market economy size structure and did not differ much, if at all, from the Western countries in this respect. A comparison of the Czech Republic and Austria (OECD, 1996) and various other country studies give partial support to the larger picture in Table 2.2. One gathers a similar perception from Table 2.1, where shares in aggregate employment are presented for Western national economies and the three transition countries in question.

However, the shares of the entrepreneurial firms in aggregate output and employment may not reflect accurately, or, to put it more precisely, may not reflect completely, the extent of the catching-up process in this respect. What matters are not only the proportions but also the density of the small and middle-sized firms, reflected in their number per thousand of population, per unit (say $1 billion) of GDP, or in another indicator of density, allowing us to gain a comparative perspective. Such indicators tend to signal whether there is a dense enough network of firms ready to undertake expansion or the new tasks of supplying old large firms, supporting them in modernizing their production profile, or cooperating with new large firms, establishing themselves as *de novo* firms in a given national economy. Interestingly, such indicators have scarcely been developed, regardless of an enormous amount of empirical research on transition. In those few that are exceptions to that attitude (see, Benacek and Zemplinerova, 1994; Zemplinerova, 1997) it has been calculated that successful transition economies by and large caught up with the density of SMEs in Western Europe. More about the entrepreneurial density later in this chapter.

Fourth, the special interest in the new, entrepreneurial private sector has been closely associated with some other related considerations of the author. In a series of articles I stressed the crucial role of the relative dynamics of the new private sector and the privatized sector as the most important determinant of economic performance in transition. Higher than elsewhere, the rate of

Table 2.2 Share of SMEs in manufacturing output in selected OECD countries ranked from the largest to the smallest share in the late 1990s (in percentages)

Country	Share in % of the total
Italy	54.8
Greece	54.1
Portugal	53.3[a]
Austria	44.0
Japan	43.0[a]
Belgium	40.6[a]
Turkey	39.7
United Kingdom	36.9
Sweden	35.8
Finland	30.2
USA	14.3[b]
Memorandum item:	
Poland	38.1[c]
Czech Republic	37.5
Hungary	36.7

Sources: Calculated from OECD Small and Medium Enterprises Outlook, 2000. For Hungary: State of Small and Medium Sized Business in Hungary, 1999. For Poland: Chmiel, 2000.

Notes: Output in firms employing up to 249 persons. Indicated separately if calculated otherwise.
a Output in firms employing up to 199 persons.
b Output in firms employing up to 99 persons.
c Output in industry (mining, manufacturing, and utilities).

economic growth of the Polish economy in the first decade of transition, as well as its earlier recovery from "transformational recession" has been – in my opinion – largely determined by the internal composition of the Polish private sector. More precisely, by the much higher share of the new private sector *vis-à-vis* that of the privatized ex-SOEs (see, *inter alia* Winiecki, 1996, 1999, and 2000b).

What I posit here largely repeats the arguments formulated earlier (Winiecki, 1999 and 2000b). Thus, not all private firms behave in the same manner in the transition economy, especially in the short to medium run, say, three to seven years. In *de novo* private firms the structure of ownership reflects the requirements of the capitalist market economy. So do the relations between owner(s) and management if they are not the same person, as is usually the case in SMEs (the relations in question concern, then, about 15 percent of the larger firms from among the aggregate SME population).

Industrial relations, those between the management and employees, are based on the understanding and acceptance of the market rules of the game. Old communist working habits are not carried *en masse* into the new firms. Individual cases of sloppy workmanship and other evident transgressions (quite frequent in the early years of *de novo* firms) are quickly reacted to and result in quick dismissals.

By contrast, old management, or even new management, in privatized SOEs tends to tolerate, at least temporarily, the survival of the old patterns of behavior. Nearly everything remains outwardly the same, except, maybe, for the work style of a few expatriate managers brought in by a new owner (if there is one).

Taking it easy on the job, shirking, stealing, and other highly adverse features characteristic of SOEs under the communist system disappear rather slowly. The same workers who often relatively quickly adapt to new requirements in *de novo* firms persevere with their old habits if they continue to work in the same, even if by now privatized, ex-SOEs. These habits are reinforced by their observation that others behave in the same manner, without much pressure from the immediate superiors (more often than not the same as in the old communist days).

The period of adjustment, of instilling new (in fact, old, but long-forgotten) work ethics, lasts for some time, even in those ex-SOEs that were taken over by a strategic investor. The story is even worse in those ex-SOEs which were privatized without such owner(s).

The foregoing is well supported empirically. Havrylyshyn and McGettigan, (1999) who surveyed most of the theoretical/empirical literature on privatization, distilled from their survey the ranking of efficiency of firms operating in the transition economy. Across the board *de novo* private firms perform best. SOEs perform worse than privatized firms, while among privatized firms insider-owned firms perform worst among privatized firms, but still better than SOEs. State enterprises are at the bottom of the performance ladder. Country studies usually confirm the pattern described above (see, e.g., Pinto *et al.*, 1993, and Jarosz, 2000, for Poland or Simoneti *et al.*, 2000, for Slovenia).

As noted in Winiecki (2000b), Poland's case has been one of rapid privatization "from below" and slow privatization "from above." It was, in a way, unique among post-communist economies in transition, including the successful ones. However, it is not only countries with the Polish pattern of privatization that may benefit from the rapid expansion of the new private firms, because a significant share of the latter in the aggregate output of the private sector positively affects the dynamism of *every* transition economy. The other two economies considered at length here, the Czech Republic and Hungary, also registered a strong expansion of the new entrepreneurial private sector, as well as for Slovakia. The data say the same on Estonia (data for the Czech Republic and Estonia, see Jurajda and Terrell, 2002). Other successful transition economies seem to follow the same pattern.

We should, then, consider more systematically linkages between the varied, large or small, presence of the new private sector and economic performance. From among the four special, transition-related, reasons for our interest in the new private sector, linkages between the new entrepreneurial private sector and economic dynamism are of particular interest here.

Alternative "stylized facts"' scenarios: new private sector and patterns of recession, recovery and expansion

The author posits that the difference in performance between the new private sector and the privatized sector is of greatest importance in the short-to-medium run. The foregoing statement requires some additional explanations, though. The view of this author is that the performance difference considered in the preceding section tends to subside over time. Workers and (old) managers adapt, with smaller or greater effort, to the performance requirements of the standard capitalist firm. The process of adjustment is expected to be faster in firms taken over by (largely foreign) strategic owners and slower in other cases, where expatriate managers, extensive training at home and abroad, and other contributions are not available to the same extent as in subsidiaries of multinational enterprises or even smaller foreign firms. In the worst cases, where adjustment is resisted too strongly or for too long, privatized firms, if not acquired in time by outside owner(s), will simply be forced to exit the market.

One way or the other, after some three to seven years since the start of transition the behavioral characteristics of firms, their industrial relations, etc., will not differ all that much across the different types of privately owned firms. Of course, by this mean private firms of the same legal form (they will continue more permanently to differ between different forms of private ownership). Therefore, consequences for performance of the division between new private and privatized firms are expected to decline or disappear as well. The relative size of the new private sector and privatized sector will cease to matter so much.

At the start of transition, however, the differences may be large, even decisive for the success or failure of the transition process. In order to explain how this impact is exercised and what are its output effects, let us present the "stylized facts"-based alternative scenarios of output change in post-communist transition.

One such path would describe economies with a relatively large and dynamic new private sector, while another would present economies where the size of the new private sector is relatively small, or even marginal. As in all such "stylized facts" scenarios, they may differ from actual, more nuanced, developments because, for expository purposes, they deliberately over-emphasize differences.

The two paths are presented respectively in Figure 2.2A and 2.2B. The stylized economy with the fast-growing and increasingly large new private sector in Figure 2.2A registers sharp output fall at the start of transition, when old demand – reflecting distorted incentives under the communist system – shrinks dramatically and the state enterprises face new, market-based demand. Consequently, they slash inventories, cut investment, and (often without much initial success) try to adjust to the requirements of the market.

The new private sector starts from scratch, as in the Czech Republic, or else it fast increases its size from the insignificant share it held under the communist system (as in Poland and Hungary). In two to three years the new private sector reaches the critical mass; it becomes large enough to strongly influence aggregate output. Therefore, within the said period, it changes increasingly significantly the path of aggregate output.

The state enterprise sector (SOE) continues, of course, to reduce output and employment (in Poland, for example, it stopped shrinking in the sixth year of transition). At a certain point the new entrepreneurial private sector begins to add more to aggregate output than state enterprise sector subtracts from it and, consequently, the aggregate output levels off and starts growing. Both paths of the state sector's output and the new private sector's output are shown in parallel with the aggregate output path in Figure 2.2A. The transformational recession is over and recovery begins. It is not yet an end to the adjustment of SOEs and privatized ex-SOEs, but their continuing adjustment does not result in aggregate output fall anymore.

With the passage of time the privatized sector begins to add net to aggregate output (see the respective output paths), while SOE sector shrinks even faster. The shrinkage in question, however, is then less due to the continuing fall of output *per* enterprise, but more to the effect of a shift of more and more enterprises from the state enterprise sector to the privatized sector. With both components of the private sector – new private and privatized – adding now to output (but usually only new private sector adding to employment) the recovery phase turns into expansion.

As we could see, the early recovery – in the third or fourth year of transition – is almost fully dependent on the dynamics of the new private sector. The SOE sector continues to shrink, the privatized sector is at that point still subtracting from aggregate output rather than adding to it, and it is only the new private sector that adds significantly to output and employment. The most detailed statistics on changing shares of the new private and privatized sector in the early transition are shown in Chapter 5 concerning Poland.

A. Output path with a large new private sector.

**B. Stylized alternative output paths in transition:
Output path with a small new private sector.**

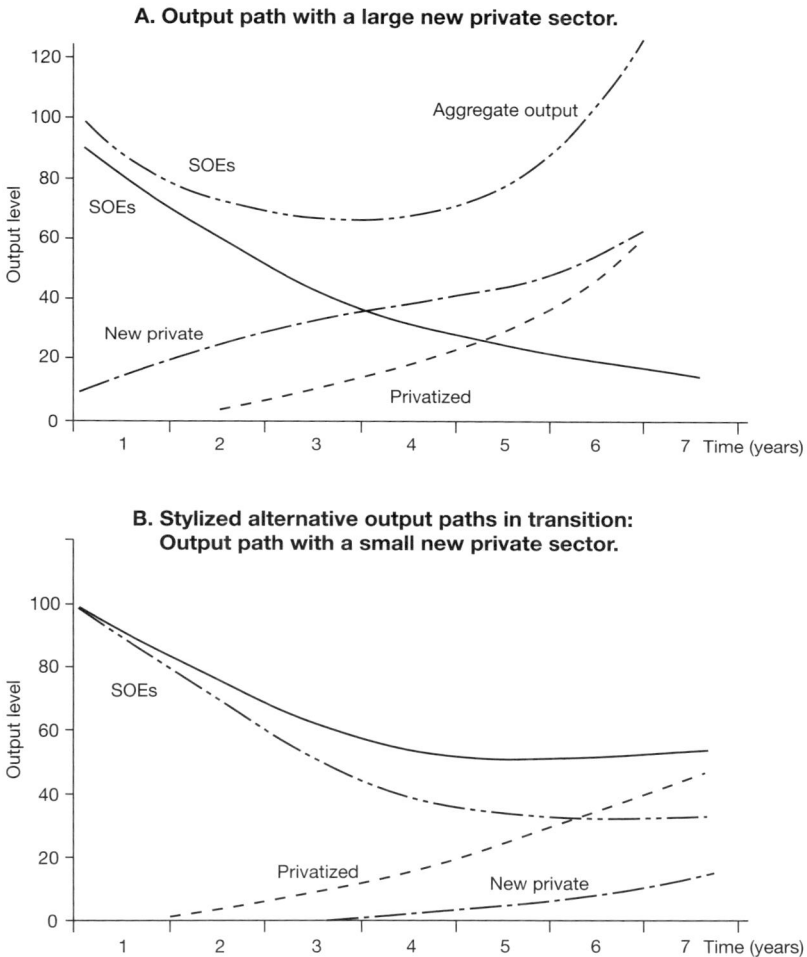

Figure 2.2 Stylised facts alternative output paths in transition.

But what happens if the new private sector does *not* display the robust growth described earlier? If some barriers, not yet analyzed, make it small or even irrelevant as a factor contributing to the recovery from transformational recession? Then, the second "stylized facts"-based output path will be observed. That output path is shown in Figure 2.2B.

Some of the processes described in the first scenario take place in roughly the same manner. The SOE sector faces the same constraint of the disappearing distorted demand pattern from the communist past and, as a result, cuts output. It is a *rough* similarity, though. It should be noted that successful transition countries liberalize radically and at the same time try to stabilize the economy. Therefore, the fall in demand by the (partly) adjusting producers and (fully) adjusting consumers is steeper in these countries.

In those countries which for reasons to be discussed did *not* succeed in generating the rapid expansion of the new private firms, both liberalization and stabilization measures are less decisive and less extensive. No watershed – a perception of the decisive break with the past – is perceived by economic agents. Therefore, their adjustment steps are more hesitant and less coherent. The past patterns of behavior exert stronger pressure on their decision processes. In consequence, the downward output adjustment in early transition is less than in the case considered earlier.

Another process, that of privatization "from above", may proceed slowly or rapidly. In either case the net contribution to output of the privatized sector is negative in the short run. In the case of rapid privatization "from above" it begins to be substantial in the medium run (at the cost of a faster fall in the share of the SOE sector).

Neither of the two processes, however, is able to reverse the path of falling output in the short to medium run. Aggregate output might have fallen more slowly in early transition than in the case described in Figure 2.2A, but it lasts much longer than in successful transition economies.

At the same time, the slowly growing entrepreneurial sector does not generate enough output and employment to match the continuing losses of the state enterprise sector plus privatized sector. The aggregate output path in Figure 2.2B reflects the foregoing by showing continuing decline over both the short- and medium-term period. The role of the new private sector which is, once again, decisive for the recovery and expansion of output during the first three to seven years of transition is clearly presented in Figure 2.2B as well.

Old state enterprises, whether privatized or not, are unwilling or unable all by themselves to adjust fully to the new requirements of the market. And they do not feel the competitive pressure of the multitude of new private firms that would force them to make a greater adjustment effort. Thus, they continue to cut output and, with a lag, to adjust downward their employment, tending toward the low-level equilibrium at the enterprise level and – in the absence of the new private sector – also at the national economy level.

The recovery, if any, is shallow. The output of the combined state and privatized sector stops declining at some point and edges upward, getting little or no boost from the new private sector. Expansion, understood here as a fast GDP growth sustained over a number of years, does not take place at all. Note that, for example, in Ukraine output continued to fall for a whole decade. A return to the output level from the pre-transition period (whatever that means in real terms, given the distorted communist statistics) is not attained. Nor does it look attainable even in the longer run.

Performance of the new private sector: the explanatory framework

Levels of analysis

As we shall see in the next section, the stylized scenarios have their clearly distinguishable real-life references. "Success stories" of transition were very close to the first scenario. Poland, Hungary, the Czech Republic, and – also chronologically – Estonia, Latvia, Slovakia, or Lithuania displayed the much-needed dynamism of their new private sector. At the same time transition laggards were much closer to the second scenario. Romania, Bulgaria, Russia, or Ukraine were unable to create enabling conditions for the expansion of the new private sector.

However, before we turn to the real-life developments concerning the role of the new private sector, this author would suggest first looking for the determinants of the different – often sharply different – performance. In other words I suggest an inquiry into the wealth and poverty of nations undergoing post-communist transition.

In line with the economic philosophy of the author, the search will concentrate on institutions. For it is institutions that overwhelmingly explain performance differentials in the face of identical supplies of production factors and inputs.

In the inquiry this author starts with the traditional levels of analysis – specific rules and general rules – that are also applied in the studies of transition. However, apart from these two levels of analysis I decided to add a third level, namely the level of meta rules, or civilizational fundamentals. For it is not only the recent past, i.e. the communist system, that influences performance. A more distant, pre-communist past plays, as we shall see, an even more important role.

Thus, the enabling conditions conducive for the establishment and expansion of the new private sector are identified at three levels of analysis:

- At the low level, which comprises the specific, detailed rules, often affecting primarily a class of economic agents (here SMEs);
- At the intermediate level of general rules (and policies pursued within the general rules), affecting the major components of transition: stabilization, liberalization, and privatization; and
- At the high level, which goes beyond economic issues and comprises

the evolving civilizational fundamentals of a wider economic, social, and political nature.

The author posits that the strength of the influence increases with each level. Observant readers may note that this author did not enumerate the legacy of the more recent, communist past as a separate factor; in contrast to a more distant past shaping civilizational fundamentals. This approach stands in sharp contrast with Chapter 1 on transformational recession. However, in transformational recovery it is a new class of economic agents, i.e. the new private sector, which contributes decisively to aggregate output recovery (or the lack of it). And the new private sector is not burdened by the distorted behavioral traits inherited from communism.

Enabling conditions and specific rules

There is no doubt that specific, detailed rules may influence economic performance, here the new private sector's performance. As Hernando de Soto (1989) had proven in the case of Peru, a mass of detailed rules may throttle economic activity to such an extent that half of the nation's labor force, entrepreneurs and workers alike, is forced to operate beyond the rules, in the "gray" economy.

Specific rules may be disaggregated into two basic categories: rules concerning establishment and those concerning operation, or functioning, of the firm. Since the latter category comprises incomparably larger set of rules (and policies concerning their application), any studies concerning specific rules of operation are necessarily limited, either in terms of the extent or the depth of the study. Unsurprisingly, then, more comprehensive studies of detailed rules can more often be found with respect to the rules of establishment.

The most important characteristics of good rules of establishment are the simplicity, parsimony, and transparency of the procedures required, the speed of operation of the organizations involved in screening procedures, and the cost of going through the process of establishment. Djankov *et al.* (2000) completed a large-scale, detailed study of the regulation of entry, covering 75 countries. The study covers, *inter alia*, most of the transition countries. Given the foregoing, we have the opportunity to look at the transition economies in comparative perspective: first, how they compare between themselves and, second, how they compare with mature market economies. Before we look at the numbers and try to make them meaningful, a word about the debate on the causes of regulation is in order. As stressed in the theoretical part of the Djankov *et al.* study, there are alternative theories of regulation found in the literature.

Traditional neoclassical ("Pigouvian") theory holds that regulations are imposed to correct numerous market failures. Extensive governmental (or government-mandated) screening is aimed at making sure that demanders receive the product or service of the required quality from the properly screened suppliers. By Pigouvian standards, then, more regulation is correlated with socially superior outcomes.

An alternative theory or theories look at the regulation from the public choice, or more widely rent-seeking, perspective. Regulations tend to be imposed primarily to benefit politicians and bureaucrats who use them for offering political favors and enriching themselves. The extensive screening of entrants makes entry costly and keeps many potential competitors out and benefits insiders who have already paid their bribes and now obtain supernormal profits (see, de Soto, 1989). By the public choice standards more regulation clearly means less socially desirable outcomes.

Djankov *et al.* call the alternative theories the "helping hand" and the "grabbing hand" – and they stress the strong support of the data for the latter. More regulation of entry is *not* associated empirically with higher quality of products, better environmental standards, etc. It is associated, though, with higher corruption, a larger gray economy, and other undesirable social and economic phenomena.

Having said the foregoing, the author will proceed further on the principle that extensive regulation is, on the average, an undesirable phenomenon and, therefore, more entry screening, longer time spent on it, and attendant higher cost are disadvantageous for the formation rate of *de novo* firms. From that perspective, looking at the data supplied by Djankov *et al.*, we may say that our successful transition countries are roughly in the middle third of the surveyed sample. Out of 75 countries, Poland is calculated to be 28th–29th, Hungary 45th, and the Czech Republic 51st.

Among European transition countries, best placed are Slovenia (12th) and Latvia (15th). The ranking is based on this author's calculations, as Djankov *et al.* did not calculate an aggregate indicator for the number of procedures, the time needed for their completion, and the cost of establishment in terms of a percent of annual GNP *per capita*, taken together.

For the record, the first places are occupied by Anglo-Saxon countries, followed by Scandinavian ones. The "core" European Union countries are spread across the whole spectrum, with Belgium (13th) and Germany (26th) at the top and France (59th) and Austria (67th) at the bottom of the group. The ranking of selected countries is found in Table 2.3.

As an important aside we may note that the Djankov *et al.* (2000) study suggests a particular view on the phenomenon of excessive business regulation and excessive welfare regulation, often called Eurosclerosis. Since continental European Union members spread across the whole range, from

Table 2.3 Selected countries ranked in accordance with ease of entry (on the basis of three indicators: number of procedures, time spent registering, and cost as percent of GNP *per capita*)

Rank	Country
	First ten countries:
1	Canada
2	New Zealand
3	Australia
4	United States
5	Sweden
6	United Kingdom
7	Denmark
8	Finland
9	Norway
10	Ireland
	European transition economies:
12	Slovenia
15	Latvia
19	Bulgaria
23	Ukraine
28–29	Poland
37	Romania
39	Lithuania
45	Hungary
48–49	Slovakia
51	Czech Republic
54	Croatia
63	Russia

Source: Own calculations on the basis of data in: Djankov *et al.*, 2000.

Note: No data on Estonia were published in the source.

the second (Belgium) to the seventh decile (Austria), Eurosclerosis should be seen as a result of a social philosophy applied at a country level, rather than overregulation applied at the European Union level. The conclusions drawn from the above study are reinforced by the results of the European Business Survey (2002) of small and medium-sized enterprises. There, domestic rules are seen to be much more often a barrier to performance than the common EU rules.

As stressed already, we do not have similar comprehensive surveys of the rules affecting the operations of firms. This is understandable, since so many operations affect performance. However, in theoretical terms, the same principle applies: more regulation means higher barriers, and higher barriers mean worse performance.

With respect to the regulatory framework concerning the operations of business firms, the concerns of new firms, and by the same token the existence of high barriers, are captured by various country studies and business opinion surveys therein. In a series of country studies on transition economies, including the economies under particular consideration in this book (see Balcerowicz *et al.* (eds), 1999), the barriers identified most often by entrepreneurs were in almost all of them the same:

- A very high burden of taxes and social security contributions (the latter 50–100 percent higher in terms of their share in GDP than in West European welfare states); and
- Excessive regulation, frequent changes in the regulatory regime, and its lack of transparency.

These two types of barrier have invariably obtained the highest rankings on the lists of existing barriers in Poland, Hungary, and the Czech Republic listed by entrepreneurs surveyed. In fact, the study referred to above also presented surveys for Lithuania and Albania, and, unsurprisingly, they gave similar results. What Kihlgren (2003) calls "convoluted legislation," as well as obstructive regulatory regime and high taxes, is also seen as barriers to entrepreneurship in Russia. These barriers may, then, be seen as near-universal for new entrepreneurial firms in the transition economies (and probably in all underdeveloped and/or distorted economies the world over).

It should be noted that the third barrier, or a set of barriers, have, also uniformly, been financial barriers. Consequently, it becomes clear why the tax burden has been stressed by almost all entrepreneurs surveyed, regardless of the nominal tax rates. Since small and middle-sized firms are by their very nature at a disadvantage in terms of obtaining external (bank) financing (see, e.g., Luczka, 2001), retained profits play a much larger role in SMEs than in large firms (see, *inter alia*, Part II in this book, as well as Kondratowicz and Maciejewski, 1996, Balcerowicz *et al.* (eds), 1999, and others). Therefore, high direct taxes, corporate and personal, strongly reduce the opportunities of SMEs for expansion.

It is posited here that not only high taxes but also extensive regulation are more costly for small and middle-sized firms than for the large ones. The latter relationship has already been subjected to some empirical verification. In a study of the Netherlands it has been established that the cost of compliance with the regulations was, e.g., almost six times higher in firms with less than ten employees than in those with more than 100 employees: roughly $3,500 vs. $600 (see Stein *et al.*, 1995).

Thus, the Laffer curve of regulation, drawn in Figure 2.3, presents two peak points (the shift to the right of each produces the decline in performance).

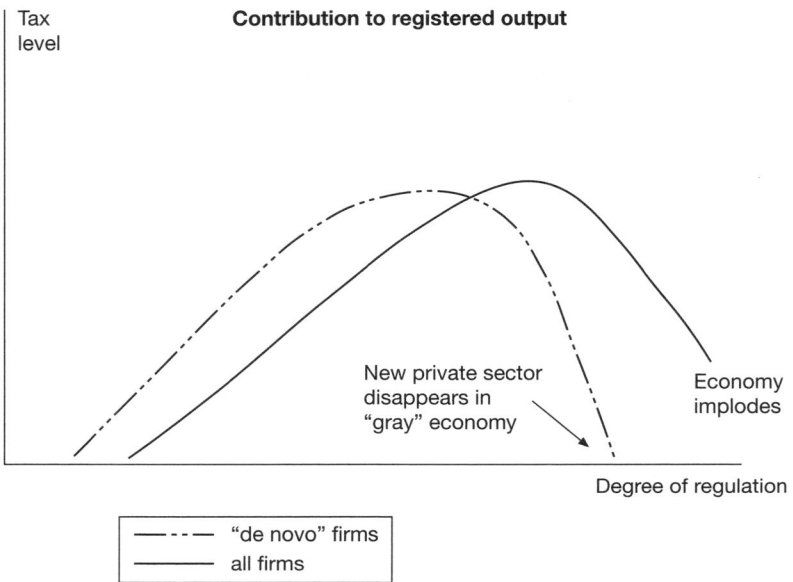

Figure 2.3 Laffer curve of regulation showing stronger impact on *de novo* private firms.

One peak point is for the population of all firms, and another, substantially to the left of the former, is for the population of SMEs. Given the higher costs and other barriers more strongly affecting smaller than larger firms, the performance of SMEs begins to weaken much earlier under the impact of the same set of rules for all firms.

The higher cost of regulation, with its performance consequences, applies not only to compliance costs, but to all costs related to regulation, including corruption costs. The study of corruption undertaken by the EBRD, covering transition economies revealed, unsurprisingly, that the "bribe tax" (payments to officials) take a substantially higher share of annual revenues in small firms than in medium and large firms. The ratio between the relative size of the bribes paid by small and by large firms is more than 2 to 1 (see Figure 2.4).

The detailed regulatory framework clearly matters and *all* transition economies would greatly benefit from reduced levels of taxation and liberalization of their regulatory regimes. Such measures could accelerate economic growth in the successful countries, while they could make a difference between success and failure in the laggard ones.

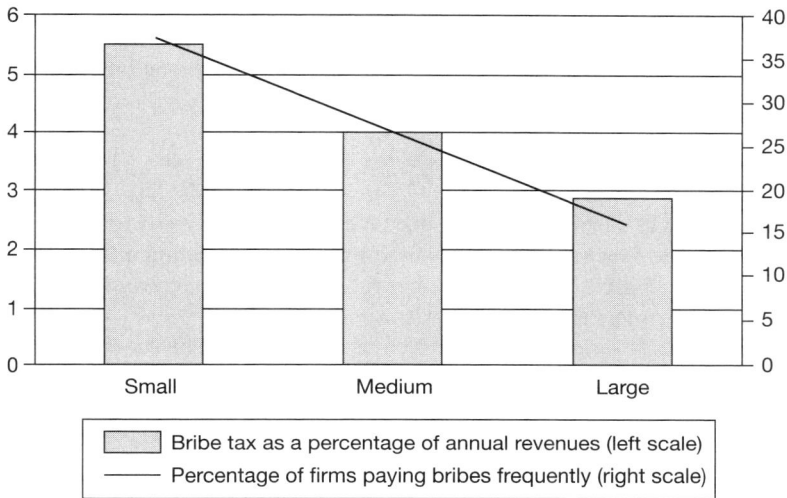

Figure 2.4 The impact of the "bribe tax" depends on the firm's size.
Source: Transition Report, 1999 EBRD.

The foregoing statement is put in conditional terms, for in line with our earlier thesis, we stress that the liberal rules of establishment and operation of firms, however important, may not be decisive for creating a conducive framework for the new entrepreneurial private sector. In other words they create necessary but not sufficient conditions for success.

We are helped in our considerations by the data from the Djankov *et al.* (2000) study. For example, Ukraine or Bulgaria have a higher rank than Poland, Hungary, or the Czech Republic, with respect to ease of entry. And yet there is no doubt that the new private sector has been contributing much more to the aggregate output in the latter three than in the former two countries. Clearly other factors affect Ukraine more adversely as it has registered almost the worst performance in terms of its transformational recession path and the meager size of its new private sector.

One, undoubtedly partial, explanation is at hand. According to another study, 64 percent of prospective entrepreneurs pay on the average an equivalent of $186 to have the registration of a firm done in an expeditious manner (Kaufman and Kaliberda, 1996). Other activities require no less frequently extorted bribes (the range of frequency is 56 percent to 97 percent).

But corruption is itself a product of an unfinished or distorted transition program, creating opportunities for the bureaucracy to demand bribes, and, at a more general level, a consequence of the weak tradition of moral order and law in a given society. The rule of law was very weak in historical Russia (to say nothing of the Soviet Union). And relentless communist pressure caused frequent replacement of the traditional moral order by what Soviet dissident Zinovyev called "technical rules of survival."

Enabling conditions and general rules: the "holy trinity" of transition

Thus, it may be restated that the success story of the new entrepreneurial private sector does not depend solely on the specific, detailed rules. It is dependent to a greater extent on other factors, as stressed already by this author (see Winiecki, 1999 and 2000b).

The previous statement is rarely contested. Many analysts agree, and empirical studies support the view nearly uniformly, that progress in the implementation of a transition program, equivalent to the well-known Hayekian *general rules*, matters. Progress in implementing the "Holy Trinity" of transition, i.e. stabilization, liberalization, and privatization measures, has been seen as the key to success. It is carefully studied by various international institutions (such as, for example, the World Bank and EBRD) and by individual analysts.

Many more or less useful indicators have been developed to measure progress in this respect, and, although one might argue to what extent some of those measures indeed measure what their inventors think they measure, one thing is certain. Imprecise as they may be, they roughly measure the actual degree progress toward the capitalist market order.

Fast aggregate institutional progress is tantamount in real-life cases to the choice of fast-track (or "big bang", or "shock therapy") strategy. The institutional laggards chose a more gradual approach, or simply did little that was required. But the consequence was that they also performed much worse in terms of economic progress.

The closer to the market system the transition countries have been, the better their performance. Coefficients of institutional progress in transition correlate positively with actual economic progress, as measured by GDP growth, inflation decline, foreign trade dynamics and structure, and other measures of economic performance.

A comparison of Table 2.4, which presents the EBRD ranking of institutional performance (Transition Report, 2000), with what we know about performance of transition economies confirms the foregoing. The countries with higher values of aggregate institutional performance indicators are at the same time best in terms of economic performance (contrary to the assertions in a number of studies hostile to transition to the capitalist market economy, e.g., most recently many authors in McIntyre and Dallago (eds), (2003)).

Table 2.4 Entrepreneurial density in selected transition economies: measured by number of entrepreneurs per 1,000 persons in the population in the second half of the 1990s

Country	Year	Ratio
Czech Republic	1998	139
Hungary	1998	64
Poland	1998	59
Slovakia	1998	56
Slovenia	1998	32
Romania	1998	15
Russia	1996	6

Sources: Winiecki, 2000b.

The considerations presented here may be called mainstream in the study of transition. However, it is at this point that the path of inquiry of the author parts with that of mainstream transition analysts. For in my opinion a study of specific and general rules of post-communist transition do not exhaust an inquiry into the relative success or failure of nations in creating enabling conditions for the establishment and expansion of the new private sector.

The contributing impact of institutions goes far beyond both the detailed regulatory framework of establishment and operation of the new private firms and the successful pursuit of the "Holy Trinity" of transition. An in-depth institutional analysis is required as well. To accomplish the task, analysts have to turn to the historical foundations of Western civilization.

Enabling conditions and historical fundamentals

Economic performance, and even systemic change itself, have been strongly influenced by broader, historically evolving fundamental economic, social, and political phenomena. Therefore, our inquiry must also look into this broader framework of liberty, law and order, and trust. The following points are an elaboration on the author's earlier articles (particularly, Winiecki 2000a).

- First, freedom of entrepreneurship, as embodied in the enabling regulatory framework, is important for all market participants. It is very important for the new participants, who bear the disproportionate cost of any barrier to entry and expansion (relative to larger, already established firms). However, *economic* liberty, embodied in the liberal regulatory framework, even if necessary for good performance of *de novo* firms, is not sufficient to make the environment really conducive for the entrepreneurs.

The framework of economic liberty should necessarily interact with, or be embedded in, a much broader framework of liberty, including civic and political liberties. It is that wider framework of liberty, rather than more narrowly conceived freedom of entrepreneurship, that underpins the entrepreneurship-friendly environment. The latter is needed to give actual and potential entrepreneurs the assurance of broader stability, understood, *inter alia*, as safety from any later persecution for their earlier pursuance of profit through the lawful operations of a private firm.

This is a minimum requirement, but a *vital* minimum in the part of the world where private profit-seeking had been for decades legislated to be a crime. Even later, when the constrained private sector was allowed to exist in some areas of the economy, it continued to be touted as the symbol of evil (and was discriminated against). The assurance of stability is needed all the more so, since entrepreneurial success often breeds envy and discrimination (at times even persecution).

Incidentally, it is the lack of such assurance that condemned to failure attempts to revive private entrepreneurship under East European "reform communism" (see Winiecki, 1991, and 1997a). No constitutional rules or policy pronouncements (the proverbial "green light" declared from time to time by communist rulers) helped the regimes to generate the dynamic expansion of the generic private sector. The would-be entrepreneurs perceived that the communist rulers simply *were not credible* and the entrepreneurial response has been, generally, very limited. Where it did take place it was usually distorted, as most of the registered effort went into activities that did not require much investment, nor a long period for pay-off.

A comparison of the rate of formation of new firms in the pre-transition and early transition period shows a striking difference with the communist past. When the emergence of political and civic liberties have been widely acknowledged by the population, the dynamics of establishment and expansion of new firms accelerated sharply in the countries under consideration (see Part II, Chapters 4 and 5, on Hungary and Poland).

- Second, well-designed and efficiently enforced property rights are an important goal of every transition program, albeit realized so far to varying extents (and even in the best performing countries it leaves much to be desired (see the EBRD Transition Report 1999)). To be more precise, it matters whether there are gains forgone, when some sophisticated types of business deals will not be entered into, given the unclear, imprecise, or even conflicting rules or their weak enforcement. But it matters even more that many more numerous, standard business transactions are not entered into because economic agents perceive that their businesses – and they themselves! – are not protected due to the inefficient and corrupt law and order regime.

Thus, however important the property rights regime may be for enhancing economic development in general and the expansion of the entrepreneurial sector in particular, it is too narrow an interpretation of the enabling institutional framework, protecting the property of economic agents. The perception of the existence of an efficient law and order regime is, then, yet another prerequisite of the successful establishment and expansion of the new private sector.

Wherever and whenever law and order is absent, due to the weakness of the (otherwise highly activist) state in its pursuit of its fundamental task as a provider of law and order, transaction costs rise enormously. If the property can easily be stolen or damaged by criminal elements operating with near impunity, then the best-designed property rights rules will not spur much entrepreneurship (except in pathological forms). Russia is a good example here (see below).

- Third, and finally, it is important that *trust* develops over time as honesty becomes increasingly rewarded through repeated business deals with those individuals whose reputation for honest dealing becomes established. The capitalist market economy is particularly well suited to develop that kind of trust, given the concordance of the structure of incentives with reputation-enhancing behavior.

What is also needed, however, is a dose of trust that is not so much the outcome of the interaction of the market (stressed earlier in this chapter), but an ingredient underpinning the emergence of a market, if the latter is to operate at the low transaction cost levels. Such general trust is more a consequence of the protracted existence of *civil society*, that is the ability and willingness of citizens or inhabitants, to organize themselves for the joint pursuit of various common goals. The interaction across political, religious, and other divides teaches them cooperative behavior and makes them more ready to accept the duties needed for the advancement of various, non-exclusive, goals.

Such "social capital" (in Putnam's terms) or "public good human capital" (in Olson's terms), or simply trust (in Fukuyama's terms) is usually low in societies emerging from the communist anomy (compare results of surveys referred to in Lovell, 2001). However, whatever trust has been found at the start of transition, was inherited from the pre-communist past, which implies that countries embarking on the path of transition have been differently endowed with that kind of trust.

It is of great importance that those taking part in the capitalist market economy, investing their time and money, trust not only economic agents known for their good reputation, but also trust the stability of the civilizational fundamentals.

Those already in business and would-be entrepreneurs should rest assured that there is a high degree of continuity based on these fundamentals. They should expect that compromises among conflicting ideas and interests are achievable – and that electoral results will not change the regulatory and/or policy landscape overnight. The more civic interactions in pursuit of various interests have accumulated in a given society, the higher will be the general trust in the stability of the political, civic, and economic order, and, in consequence, the degree of continuity. With low trust and little prospect for continuity, the time horizon for entrepreneurs is shortened considerably and the new private sector will be both substantially smaller and oriented toward short-term gains. Both prospective outcomes are equally undesirable.

Summing up the foregoing, liberty, law and order, and trust are the civilizational fundamentals that underpin transition efforts. However well designed and consistently implemented particular transition measures may be, missing or weak fundamentals will seriously undermine the desired outcomes.

Let me offer some examples supporting the foregoing thesis. As early as in winter 1989 this author noted, while writing a new introduction to his book *Resistance to Change in the Soviet Economic System*, that clear-cut political change is a crucial signal to the present and future entrepreneurs that systemic change is real and irreversible. Wherever that signal is missing or unclear, the probability of success in accomplishing economic change would be limited (if not actually non-existent). The experience of past economic transition efforts has amply proven the point. The lingering threat of the return of communist rule in some post-Soviet (CIS) countries has been a strong deterrent to entrepreneurship, both domestic and foreign.

An example on a broader scale is based on the juxtaposition of two sets of transition economies. During my lectures on transition, while discussing civilizational fundamentals, I offer two maps (see Figure 2.5A and 2.5B). The first presents East-Central and Eastern Europe's leaders and laggards in twentieth to twenty-first-century post-communist transition. Nobody has ever contested the classification; everybody can see the difference between success and the lack of it. The second map displays the twenty-first-century divide between Western and Eastern Christendom. Here there is no arguing with facts, either.

The most surprise is when I put one map transparency upon another. For it turns out that it is roughly *the same* divide. All transition countries that are widely seen as success stories are countries of predominant or exclusive Western Christendom. This division of transition countries into two groups, leaders and laggards, has been in a way confirmed by the European Union authorities. All eight new post-communist members admitted to the EU are countries from one and the same side of the divide: Western Christendom . . . Clearly the past casts a very long shadow when it comes to the impact of institutions. As stressed already in Winiecki (1997b), the separation of temporal and transcendental authority in the West since the fourth century AD created some space for individual choices. As Landes (1998) noted "Christianity . . . early made the distinction between God and Ceasar. . . . This did not preclude misunderstandings and conflict . . ." But the benefits were very significant. Where authority is divided, dissent flourishes. This may be bad for certainty and conformity; but it is surely good for the spirit [of inquiry – J.W.] and popular initiatives."

So did later feudal decentralization of political authority, which gave an edge to the innovative. Wherever rulers put obstacles to their inventions, they could easily exercise an exit option. That meant moving to places where rulers accepted innovative craftsmen, merchants, financiers, etc. in the hope of increasing their tax volume (rather than tax level).

An even greater contribution to the uniqueness of the West came from the gradual strengthening of the position of Western cities relative to the countryside and its local *seigneurs*. The creation of many self-governing, and often fully independent, city *communes* helped to weaken political power because city governments were those of the merchants and other business people, who jealously protected their economic activities from political encroachments. These processes had been increasing (however unevenly) economic freedom. It is not surprising that in Hanseatic cities of Northern Europe the proud slogan had it that "Stadtluft macht frei."

These trends made the West very different from the rest (see, in particular, North and Thomas, 1973; Rosenberg and Birdzell, 1986; Powelson, 1994; Landes, 1998). But wherever societies have been living for centuries under one exclusive, overarching authority, as they did in Czarist Russia and other countries of Eastern Christendom, a sharply differing – and much more constrained – perspective on individualism has evolved (see, e.g., Brenner, 1990). In the Byzantine empire, the cradle of Eastern Christendom, the patriarch, head of the Church, had simply been the emperor's deputy for ideological affairs (to use a more contemporary communist terminology). That story was later repeated everywhere within Eastern Christendom.

These divisions between Western and Eastern Christendom, lasting for a thousand years, have been overlaid with the more recent influences of the corrosive communist system. This is yet another example of the impact of institutions. For the less painful were the ravages of communist moral nihilism, the less widespread the application of "technical rules of survival," and the closer the society had been to the mainstream moral order of capitalism

Figure 2.5A East-Central European and East European transforming economies.

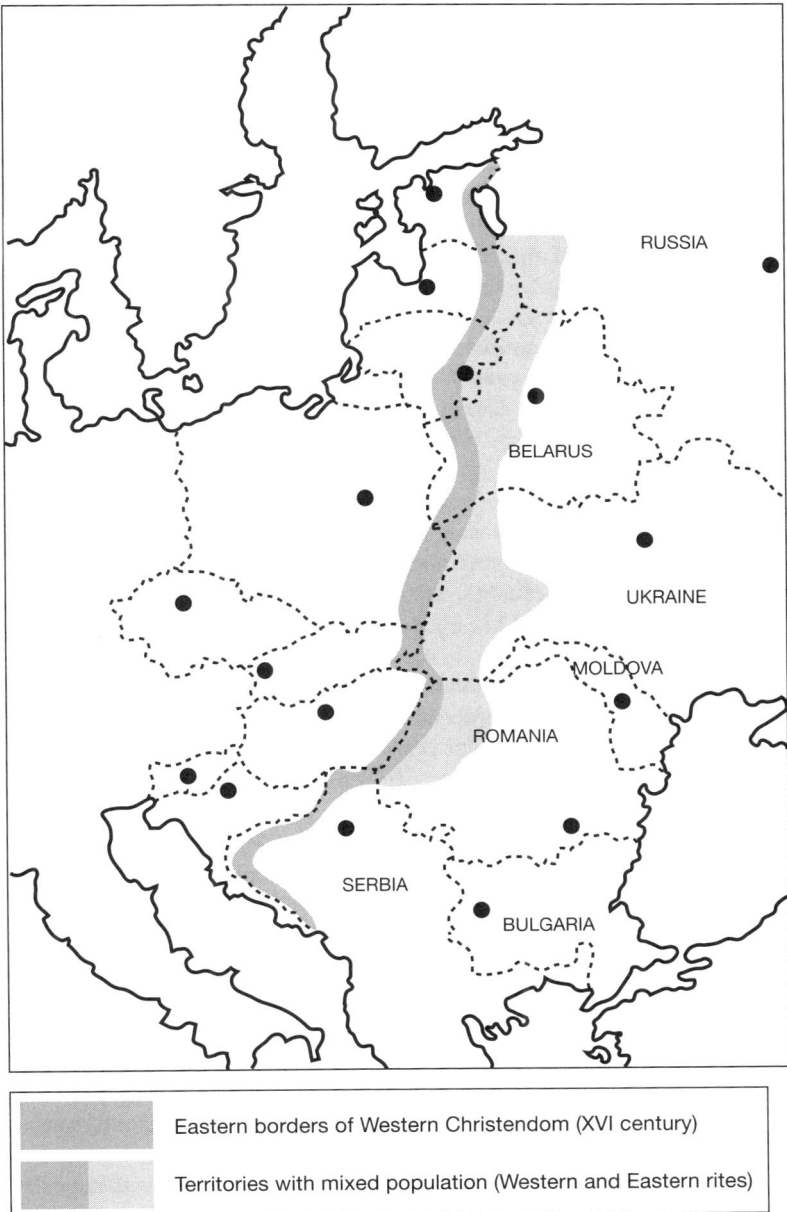

RUSSIA

BELARUS

UKRAINE

MOLDOVA

ROMANIA

SERBIA

BULGARIA

	Eastern borders of Western Christendom (XVI century)
	Territories with mixed population (Western and Eastern rites)

Figure 2.5B The East–West split in Christendom.

in pre-communist times, the faster and less costly has been the transition to liberty.

Explanations and realities

General overview

After the multilevel analysis of institutional determinants of the establishment and expansion of the new private sector, the next step will be to look at the real-life developments with respect to this crucial aspect of transition. The usual barrier is the statistical base. Realities, presented in statistical terms, have been sketchy at best, especially if we look for reliable comparative statistics. National sources have also been scarce, fragmentary, and undergoing continuous revisions and reclassifications. Even international institutions, with their sizable human and financial resources, have not been able to generate the desirable amount of sophisticated statistics on the SME sector (let alone the new private sector) and its contribution to transition.

The data on the new private sector are available to a greater extent for successful transition countries, and in particular for the Czech Republic, Hungary, and Poland, with those on Slovakia and the Baltic countries being somewhat less detailed (except for Estonia). As far as transition laggards are concerned, the data are much scarcer – one may say, in line with the scarcity of the new entrepreneurial private sector.

Thus, in Poland, Hungary, and the Czech Republic (in the early years of transition in what was still Czechoslovakia) the new private sector began to grow very rapidly in the very first years of transition, that is in the period of steep aggregate fall in demand. Regardless of the general retrenchment, new private firms expanded fast, satisfying new, market-based demand, and generating in two to three years a substantial part of aggregate output or GDP. The studies in Chapters 3–5 of this book put that share at 20–25 percent in the first few years, with the subsequent increase to 40–45 percent and sometimes more as transition entered its second decade.

As everywhere in economics there are outliers here, too. In actual fact, *one* outlier. If we assess the generally identifiable group of best performers only one country displays significant differences with the pattern described above. Slovenia, undoubtedly a good performer, registers both relatively lower aggregate share of the private sector in output and employment (see Figure 2.1, on page 45, with respect to the former), and relatively weaker dynamics of the new entrepreneurial private sector.

The privatization arrangements, affected by inherited communist Yugoslav institutional idiosyncrasies (with the workers' self-management as their corollary), generated two types of deviations from the post-communist transition pattern. First, they skewed the ownership structure of privatized firms in favor of less efficient types of private ownership, such as insider-owned firms (on a property rights approach to various forms of ownership, see Winiecki, 1992). Second, they contributed to the maintenance of the overly large public enterprise sector. All that has been kept, as shown in Simoneti *et al.* (2000), at the expense of economic efficiency.

Wherefrom stems, then, Slovenia's relatively superior economic performance? The opinion of this author is that it stems from path dependence, that is Slovene past economic development experience. In the pre-WWI Austro-Hungarian empire Slovenia had belonged to the more developed Austrian part, comprising also Czechia (presently the Czech Republic), the industrial heartland of the empire. In the inter-war period and post-WWII communist Yugoslavia, Slovenia was the most developed part of that country. Given the relative economic openness of communist Yugoslavia (relative, of course, to other communist economies), it has also been most exposed to economic competition in Western markets. Thus, it had less to adjust to in the transition period, since Slovene firms had been trading to a large extent with the West even under the old communist regime.

It is then, path dependence and the higher level of development that explain much of the good performance. They have also helped in establishing a relatively less intrusive regulatory regime (please note the 12th position, best among post-communist economies, of Slovenia in the Djankov *et al.* (2000) study). Over time, of course, as Slovene enterprises will be more and more forced to compete on equal footing with EU firms, the disadvantages of a distorted structure of ownership will become increasingly visible, while the opportunity to subsidize the inefficient SOEs will be increasingly reduced. This will exert an increasing pressure for change. For the moment, however, Slovenia lives partly on the comparative advantages inherited from the past.

Returning to generalities, in all transition leaders the fundamental requirements set forth in the preceding section have been present to a larger extent than in transition laggards. Political system change could not have been more marked. The law and order, leaving much to be desired everywhere, has been nonetheless markedly better in the former. Also, the protection of property rights has been better, while corruption is correspondingly lower.

Note that in terms of the level of the "bribe tax" and the "time tax" (that is, senior management time spent dealing with authorities) Slovenia also leads the transition economies, being least affected by these systemic distortions. Other East-Central European (ECE) success economies follow, with Hungary and Estonia doing slightly better in these respects than the Czech Republic and Poland. The five most successful countries, plus a few more from the same ECE group (including the Baltic countries), would also be those where one would expect to find relatively more trust inherited from the pre-communist past.

Altogether, at the level of systemic fundamentals, the best performers created the best enabling conditions for the establishment and expansion of the new entrepreneurial private sector (privatization "from below"). The same may be said by and large about their progress in privatization "from above". But what about evaluation at the low and intermediate levels of analysis? Ranking in accordance with the rules of establishment (entry) and operations and their impact on the new entrepreneurial private sector is a more complicated exercise, given the large variety and number of possible indicators.

Moreover, as signaled already, the *specific* arrangements may not necessarily indicate the best enabling environment for the new private sector in the absence of positive influences of higher-level determinants. The same strength of, say, tax and regulatory barriers may nevertheless be less painfully felt in the presence of, say, an increasingly stable macroeconomic framework, including falling inflation, as well as a stronger law and order regime.

The fact that, say, in the Czech Republic entry screening includes the requirement to obtain a positive opinion of the local administration, not required, e.g., in Bulgaria, puts potential entrepreneurs in the former country at a disadvantage relative to potential entrants in the latter. It is duly reflected in the lower ranking of the Czech Republic in the area of the regulation of establishment (51st position vs. 19th). But it may be compensated for by many other characteristics such as, for example, a much higher probability of Czech new private firms to obtain bank financing (and to obtain it earlier in the life of the firm) than in Bulgaria.

The comparative position of the best performers bears a similarity to the behavior of cyclists in the leading pack in, say, the Tour de France competition. At one time or another one of the cyclists comes to the fore, only to be superseded soon by another from the same pack. Occasionally, an outsider joins the leading pack for some time, but soon falls behind to the *peleton*, that is the main cyclists' group, pedaling at some distance from the leading pack. The leading pack does not feel threatened by such transient intruders.

Moving back from the cycling parable to a neo-institutional approach, the *higher level determinants are the most important*. Polish, Czech, or Hungarian entrepreneurs may complain about taxes and regulations, and rightly so, since barriers in these respects are much stronger than those for entrepreneurs from the continental EU countries, to say nothing of the Anglo-Saxons and Scandinavians. But given the more supportive fundamentals and steadier progress in stabilization, liberalization, and privatization "from above" than in transition laggards, they perform much better even under the intrusive detailed regulations.

Considerations on leaders and laggards: qualitative and quantitative differences

The gulf between good performers from East-Central Europe, stretching from Estonia in the Northeast to Slovenia in the Southwest, and the rest of the post-communist group of countries is probably best exemplified by the comparison between Poland and Russia. It has been generally agreed (until very recently) that Poland is an economic success story, while Russia is not. This is the case even if many analysts do not appreciate how very different Russia is in political-economic terms from its communist past, as rightly noted, e.g., by Mau (2000). Where analysts differ, it is usually with respect to the causes of this difference.

The mainstream explanation of Poland's success is as follows. Strong stabilization measures at the start of transition and rapid liberalization are seen as both necessary and sufficient conditions to force adjustment on the then overwhelmingly dominant state enterprise sector. Early initiated (albeit slow) Privatization "from above", when initiated early, albeit slowly, helps to shift some firms from the inefficient state sector to the efficient private sector. To a greater extent than anywhere else – except Hungary and even more, Estonia – bad performers are allowed to fail (even if actual exit drags on). The foregoing creates enabling conditions conducive to early recovery that starts in mid-1992. From then on it is, more or less, plain sailing.

There is a weak spot in this mainstream explanation, though, which may be easily noted after reading pages 49–53 of this chapter on the alternative "stylized-facts" scenarios, concerning output paths. Readers will note immediately that the mainstream explanation tells us nothing about *who generates output growth*. For even if SOEs and privatized firms adjust to the new market conditions they do not generate a net output increase in early transition (see above).

The mainstream explanations concerning Russia are the reverse of what Poland did. Thus, the stress is put on failed stabilization (with the government and the central bank working most of the time at cross purposes), on erratic and incomplete liberalization, and on the impact of the foregoing failures on privatization "from above". The privatization in question was, indeed, one of the few successes of Russia's incomplete transition. Yet stabilization and liberalization failures did not allow ownership transformation to continue. In unstable macroeconomic conditions and much microeconomic interference there were few potential buyers of Russia's firms from the incompetent owner-insiders. The necessary restructuring, leaving firms in the hands of strategic outside owners (the most efficient form of private ownership), did not take off. The result has been continuing output decline and, consequently, a greatly delayed shift from transformational recession to transformational recovery.

Again, the mainstream argument, just as in Poland's case, glosses over the same issue of who is to generate the recovery: namely, since early output recovery is not generated by state enterprises or privatized firms, but, as we know already, by new private firms, why did it matter so much that SOEs did not exit or did not become efficiently privatized?

To illustrate the point better, this author suggests the following counter-factual scenario. Let us assume that Russia started *successful* transition, that it pursued a consistent macroeconomic policy and, in consequence, increased markedly the level of price and output stability. Also, it liberalized rapidly along the same lines as Poland did. Would that, in accordance with the mainstream reasoning, ensure early recovery? My answer is NO! In Poland state enterprises' output declined for six years in row, from 1990 to 1995. At the same time the net contribution of privatized enterprises to output has been very low and most of that time negative.

The mainstream explanations on Poland or on Russia say *nothing* on the new entrepreneurial private sector. Therefore, they are unable to explain why Polish GDP stopped falling in the third year of transition, while Russian GDP fell for seven years in row, recovered slightly in 1997, and fell again the next year.

Clearly, differences between Russia and Poland must lie elsewhere. As stressed in the preceding section, the differences are between the civilizational fundamentals in both countries. To begin with the case of Russia's relative success, that is privatization "from above", Russia failed not just because macroeconomic stability had not been reached and the economy had not been liberalized enough. All that is true, but it failed also, if not primarily, because almost none of the fundamentals were present and it is these fundamentals that underpin transition measures. Without those fundamentals, including the clear-cut perception of irreversible political change and the strong enforce-ment law and order, the level of risk associated with entrepreneurship in Russia was extremely high. This affected both privatization "from above" (few outsiders ready to take over Russian insider-managed firms) and privati-zation "from below" (high risk as deterrent to entrepreneurship). The level of entrepreneurship, as evidenced by almost any indicator, was very low.

Compared to Poland, where the fundamentals may be regarded as being, more or less, present (or at a minimum stronger than in Russia), the level of Russian entrepreneurship is drastically lower. The rough measure of the number of entrepreneurs per 1,000 inhabitants in the late 1990s, presented for a number of transition economies in Table 2.4, reveals the ratio for Russia to be almost *ten times lower* than that for Poland.

Other measures, such as the share of employers and self-employed in total employment outside agriculture, show major differences, too. Incidentally, the perception of the leading pack and the rest are strengthened by the use of the indicator in Table 2.4. The Czech Republic, Hungary, Poland, and Slovakia clearly belong to the same category, with Romania and Russia registering ratios four to ten times lower. Again, Slovenia, as noted earlier, is located in between the two groups. There are no data for Ukraine about entrepreneurial density, but the comparison of the share of employers and self-employed in the total labor force shows the ratios for Hungary and Poland being about eight times higher (see Transition Report, 2000).

Incidentally, Szostkowski (2003) in his comparative statistics gives different ranking of entrepreneurial density. His approximations give Hungary, rather than the Czech Republic, the first place. But for a group as a whole, the ratio of entrepreneurs per 1,000 inhabitants in East-Central European countries is similar to the one in Table 2.4 and ranges between 100 and 40 (still much higher than in transition laggards). The comparison with the cyclists' leading pack is very apposite here again.

Russian statistics are very unreliable and students of the Russian economy argue among themselves about entrepreneurial density there (see, e.g., Radaev, 2003; Bukhvald and Vilensky, 2003; Orlov, 2003). But even the most optimistic evaluations put Russia at the bottom of the range, below ECE countries. It is only the distance from the pack that changes from one assessment to another.

There are still three issues left unanswered that require consideration here, while the author is confronting theorizing and realities. The first is a major weakness of all new private sector, or SME, data, for all post-communist economies. Namely, these data do not take into account the gray economy. The inclusion of the gray economy would in all probability reduce the yawning gap between transition hopefuls and transition laggards. This author posits, however, that the weakness in question does not matter for the crucial issues considered in this chapter.

After all, the size of the gray economy is one of *the indicators* of *failure*. Here, of failure in transition. If one were to compare the share of the gray economy across transition countries with transition progress in institutional terms, the correlation between the progress in transition and the relatively low share of the gray economy would be clearly visible.

To make the point in a more systematic manner, informal, or unregistered, entrepreneurship is an inferior form of entrepreneurship. It is, as shown forcefully in De Soto (1989), a high-cost alternative to the operation in a low-transaction-cost capitalist market economy. Informal, or gray, entrepreneurs cannot enjoy the normal benefits of a formal economy. Their ownership titles are very tenuous, they do not benefit from the existing financial system, their ability to grow is therefore very limited, and their firms are exposed to a much greater risk of extortion from those in authority. Operating in a gray economy is a defensive reaction to the emergence of the rent-seeking political class and bureaucracy that throttle or at the very least strongly constrain the opportunities for healthy economic development.

The second issue concerns explanations of lagging entrepreneurship in Russia and other less successful transition countries. We proved earlier that the mainstream explanation is silent about the dynamics of the new private sector, or even the SME sector and, consequently, its contribution to output path. But it is interesting to see whether there are alternatives to this author's ideas on the market. One such alternative is often offered by some Russian authors who suffer from the phenomenon that may be called "state worship." They stress that the Russian new private sector is underdeveloped because the state did not help in its development (see Glinkina, 2003; Radaev, 2003; Bukhvald and Vilensky, 2003; Orlov, 2003).

They look to institutionalized support measures in, say, Hungary (see, Bukhvald and Vilensky, 2003) and find the difference between success and failure in a plethora of SME support programs. What they do not notice is that there have been far fewer such programs in Poland and still fewer in the Czech Republic and yet there is no difference in entrepreneurial density among these transition leaders. Therefore, the statement (forecast?) by Orlov (2003) that "the development of small business in 2003–05 will depend on the scale of financial support it gets from the government" is tantamount to a complete misreading of the relative importance of the enabling institutional conditions and direct state intervention. "State worship" is particularly frequent in Russia, but its presence can be found elsewhere as well (see, for example, Dallago, 2003 and Kolodko, 2003).

One more case of this intellectually empty "state worship" is supplied by Radaev (2003), who presented both the dynamics of SME firms in Russia and the state support measures. Thus, he showed that except for the very early period, 1991–94, there was no growth in the number of SMEs, while state support measures started later, often much later, in the transition process. Disarmingly, he expresses his astonishment at "the paradox that the strongest increase in the sector occurred when there was virtually no such [state – J.W.] support." With his "state worshipping" worldview, he clearly does not take into account that the two developments, SME expansion and state support, may simply be (at best) uncorrelated. At best, because state intervention may not necessarily be neutral, but actually *harmful* to the activity it is expected to support.

The third issue is a variation on the theme of state support. Since many surveys of the new firms, or the SME sector, note entrepreneurs' complaints about constraints on access to the banking sector, or even about the alleged discrimination of smaller firms (see earlier in the chapter), it is of importance to give some thought to the question. In other words, do SMEs need large, varied, and sophisticated financial support programs?

In what probably is the best book on the subject, Luczka (2001) explains very well that usually there is no discrimination against smaller firms. Higher interest rates on their loans are convincingly justified by the relatively higher cost per dollar lent (higher transaction costs) and higher lending risk. What is left to do by the public authorities are some special support programs, which could relax the constraints in question (to some extent at least), without undermining the market rules of the game.

Various more or less ingenious measures have been invented and applied the world over. The problem with those measures is that it is very difficult to link them to the performance of the SME sector. The author posits that most probably cuts in personal income tax rates, combined with deregulation and debureaucratization, would generate a much better economic performance on the part of the new entrepreneurial private firms than would any financial support programs. The hypothesis, although impossible to prove directly, can be easily proven indirectly. Transition leaders, in contrast with transition laggards, not only have their civilizational fundamentals right, but also on average they register relatively lower tax and regulatory barriers among the post-communist transition countries. But this story has already been outlined on pages 55–60 of this Chapter.

Coming back, toward the end, to our juxtaposition of Poland and Russia, we may now attempt to draw real-life output paths for both countries. This we do in Figure 2.6. A comparison of the "stylized-facts"-based scenarios of output paths in the earlier Figure 2.2A and 2.2B with the actual GDP paths for Poland and Russia in Figure 2.6 confirms the strong concordance between stylized facts, based on our theorizing, and reality.

Generalizing from Poland and Russia to two groups of countries, once again leaders and laggards, the relatively successful and relatively unsuccessful, fall into two distinct groups, with the former following the Polish pattern and the latter following the Russian pattern. The indexes of real GDP for East-Central Europe (including the Baltic countries) and for the post-Soviet countries, i.e. the members of the Commonwealth of Independent States, present clearly different output paths. The GDP paths shown for these two country groups in the Transition Report (2000) do not differ from those of Poland and Russia.

In place of conclusions

Nearly everything that matters with respect to the role of the new private sector, its decisive impact on recovery and expansion, and determinants of its success or failure as an engine of the transition economy have already been presented. There is little that could usefully be added as separate conclusions from those that have been formulated earlier in the chapter.

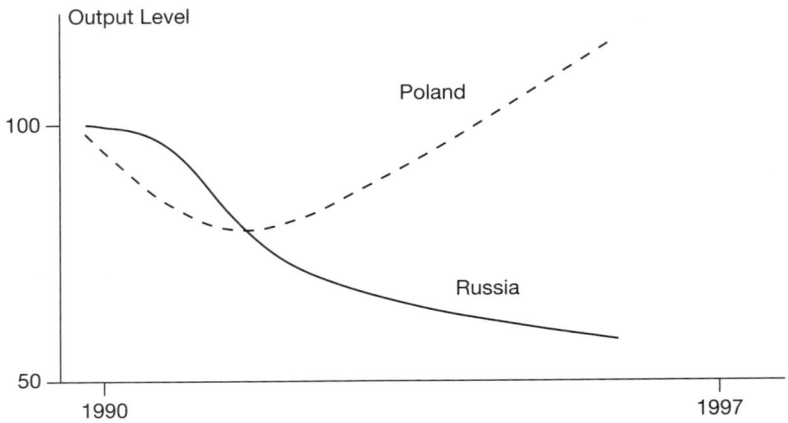

Figure 2.6 Real-life output (GDP) paths for Poland and Russia in early- to medium-term transition.

Therefore only two additional comments will be made. The hierarchy of determinants of performance of the new private sector and the dominant role of civilizational fundamentals should not absolve policy-makers from not doing their job, that is, from lowering taxes, simplifying or eliminating regulations, and generally reducing the burden of doing business for the new private sector. First, because these burdens bear much more strongly on new and smaller firms. And, second, because in quite a few good performers in transition, the tax burden, degree of overregulation, and corruption has *increased* since the second half of the 1990s as bureaucracies and politicians rediscovered the benefits of populism and rent-seeking under new market arrangements. And high taxes are positively correlated with inferior entrepreneurship, that is with the gray economy (see, Johnson *et al.*, 1998).

And, finally, there are those, like me, who believe that the political, civic, and economic liberties are not forever limited to a certain subset of countries privileged by history (see the preceding section). The author would like to stress that people, including the elites, living in the rest of the world should not feel discouraged. It is not impossible to establish free market economies, for example, on the other side of the "faultline" between Western and Eastern Christendom. It will, however, take more, maybe *much* more time than in countries where the room for individual initiative, innovation, and entrepreneurship has been so much greater for centuries.

In the meantime, being a transition laggard does not mean that the transition country is still a communist one with a superficially reformed centrally administered economy, and with a new dictator instead of a communist party secretary at the top (although sometimes it may be one and the same person). Some post-communist countries fit the foregoing definition, but fortunately only a few. As for the rest, they are simply very high transaction cost economies, on a long, bumpy, zigzagging road to political, civic, and economic liberties.

Part II

The new private sector

3 The Czech case

Vladimir Benacek

Data problems

The statistical comparison of new private firms with the old privatized firms in transition has been very difficult because state-owned and ex-state-owned large firms have continued not only to shed labor, but also to shed various activities unrelated to their core businesses. Thus, a small or medium-sized firm may be sometimes a still state-owned or privately owned entity, new only in the sense of the date of its legal establishment. In terms of intra-firm behavior of management or employees it should be classified as an old firm. On this issue, see more in Chapter 2.

In addition, new investments, acquisitions, and mergers continuously erode the borderline between the two sets of economic agents. In any case, the availability of data on both (changing) sets of economic agents has been scarce. An alternative, second-best strategy that we have taken is to compare small and medium-sized enterprises and large enterprises, assuming that *de novo* (authentic) private firms are highly correlated with SMEs, while the former, now privatized SOEs remain highly correlated with the large firms.

The latter approach also raises some methodological problems. First, the depth of statistical reports on large enterprises (over 250 employees) may differ from the reports of the medium-sized ones (from 25 to 249 employees) and the small firms. The differences can be both in the wider or narrower choice of indicators and in the quality (reliability) of reporting. Thus, the extent of biases, errors and omissions rises as the size of the firm decreases. The biggest problems are with the statistics on small firms and on the self-employed (representing together approximately 15 percent of GDP). Their statistics are based on random surveys with a reduced set of indicators, often misinterpreted. The methodology of reporting may be changing over time, too. The time series are, then, not necessarily comparable.

The statistics used by this author are based on data from 2 primary, 17 secondary and 5 tertiary industries (construction, trade, catering and hotels, transport and communication, financial sector and other services) in accordance with NACE classification for 1995 and 2000. The firms were divided into three groups. Large firms with 250 and more employees, medium-sized firms with 20-249 employees and remaining small firms, including self-employed workers. Medium-sized firms included a number of former SOEs, whose assets were separated from the large firms and privatized as an autonomous entity. Therefore, the research results for firms in the middle-sized category (20–249 employees) in some industries must be interpreted with some caution.

Another problem was that we were not able to distinguish between indigenous and foreign firms. Unfortunately, foreign-owned firms were not distributed in all three size-categories in a uniform manner (see Benacek and Zemplinerova, 1997b); the smaller the size of firm, the less presence is there of foreign-owned firms. Foreign firms were more productive and profitable than indigenous firms: their labor productivity was on the average higher by 40 percent in 1995 and by over 70 percent in 1999. Given the foregoing, some industries with intensive FDI inflows would make comparisons of domestic (indigenous) small and large firms less reliable, since the outcome might have been strongly influenced by the foreign, rather than indigenous, large or small firms.

Generalities

The economic statistics of the OECD countries for the last 20 years show that the SMEs have retained their important role in national economies, in spite of a rapid ascent of multinational enterprises (MNEs). In fact, since 1986, we have observed a rising trend in the share of SMEs in aggregate employment in most economies of the European Union. SMEs may not only provide employment to the majority of the work force but they may be in many mature market economies the most important net provider of new jobs. The network of SMEs, functioning as flexible and efficient suppliers of semi-finished products and services to large firms, has been also an essential factor behind the competitiveness of the OECD member countries on both the domestic and international markets. It is becoming accepted that there is a division of labor between the large and the small business firms (see Acs, 2003).

The preceding statement can be reformulated as a hypothesis that large and small firms have different roles to play in modern market economies. Their respective roles should be evaluated from two different points of views with respect to:

• first, the competition between them inside the same industry; and
• second, the complementarity of their functions.

As to the former, the competition on globalized world markets is subject to the dominant roles of MNEs and large domestic domestic companies. The relationship between them is theoretically explainable by oligopolistic Cournot or Bertrand adjustments of quantities of output or prices, resulting in changed market shares. The functioning of such imperfect arrangements may, however, be Pareto-improved if some outside competitors pose a potential threat to collusive behavior of dominant firms. The mechanism of competition from the side of SMEs is discussed by Pelkmans (1997).

As to the latter, the complementarity between larger and smaller firms may be explained by economies of scale. In some production lines the technologies are effectively applicable even at a family-firm scale. The advances in electronics and the expanding share of services in GDP have opened new potential areas of business activities for SMEs.

In contrast with traditional domains of SMEs (such as agriculture, most light industries, construction, and personal services) which were labor-intensive, modern domains (such as semiconductors, electronic design and testing, applied science, information, specific chemistry, healthcare, etc.), are generally both physical capital and human capital intensive. As was extensively documented in Silicon Valley, SMEs can even build on economies of scale that are external to the firm (see, *inter alia*, Porter, 1990 and Saxenian, 1994).

Another argument supporting the complementarity of SMEs and large firms is the dependence of large companies on flexible supplies (so called "backward links") that are acquired *via* outsourcing. It was confirmed recently that the importance of spillovers and networks has become a crucial condition for a growing high-wage economy. The spillovers usually flow from large firms (e.g., MNEs coming as foreign direct investors, see Blomström and Kokko (1994)) to indigenous firms, most of them SMEs. On the other hand, it is necessary that the indigenous firms do not lag too much behind MNEs in technological level, R&D, and human capital; otherwise their interaction will not lead to the desired complementarity.

To conclude, we may hypothesize that a modern high-growth economy requires the existence of the following conditions:

- A balanced "division of labor" between large firms and SMEs;
- A competitive environment, where SMEs, as fringe competitors, play nonetheless an irreplaceable role in reducing the rents aimed at by colluding oligopolies;
- A contestable environment, where SMEs have a chance to wrest a market share from firms with market power;
- An institutional environment that precludes the existence of barriers to the development of SMEs such as the burden of bureaucracy, over-regulation, etc., with its highly adverse effects, particularly on smaller firms, of high transaction costs; and

- More specifically, an institutional environment that supports the smooth functioning of:
    - financial markets, such as capital markets, banking and insurance;
    - R&D and supply of skilled labor and human capital;
    - provision of public goods and transparent rules of public procurement; and
    - law and order infrastructure.

Institutional changes in transition economies are needed in order to improve the functioning in these areas.

The above considerations omit, however, one crucial factor that is not questioned any more within Western civilization. It is now a generally accepted tenet that private ownership of capital for producing private goods is more efficient than public ownership because it has superior incentives for governance, decision-making, risk-bearing, innovation, competition and restructuring (Djankov and Murrell, 2002). Private capitalist ownership in advanced market economies developed in a gradual evolutionary process over 150 years in most Western countries. It subjected the owners and the performance of their firms to long-lasting tests of viability and it created institutions that confined the behavior of enterprises to certain standards.

Therefore, the reemergence of the private sector in transition economies has been a priority throughout the region, at least in those countries where a larger goal, that is the shift to a capitalist, market economy, has also been the priority. The private sector, however, may emerge in two complementary ways.

In order to find workable analytical concepts, we will define two typologies of the evolution of the private sector: "from above" and "from below," as stressed by Gruszecki and Winiecki (1991) and Winiecki (2000b). The first of these two methods is based on turning existing state-owned enterprises (SOEs) into private hands, for the achievement of which the activism of the government and its bureaucratic hierarchies is crucial. An alternative approach aims at creating the private sector through the establishment and expansion of *de novo* private firms. In the strategy "from below," the mainstream of activity comes from the grass roots of the economy, i.e. it takes place at level of the autonomous firm. In the latter method, it is the entrepreneurial activism of private owners that matters first and foremost.

Size, structure, and performance of *de novo* private firms

The first step in our analytical inquiry into the basic characteristics of the sector in question should be to find out how the development of *de novo* firms has proceeded since the collapse of communism in Czechoslovakia. Interest in the establishment and expansion of the Czech authentic, entrepreneurial private sector, or the SME sector, was rather low, both in terms of the intellectual and political interest, until 1997.

Note, however, that the preoccupation with voucher privatization, and generally privatization "from above" had easily explainable reasons at the time: 98.5 percent of aggregate output and employment was concentrated in the state, or "socialized," sector in 1989. Thus, the lobbying power of large enterprises apart, there were traditional, democratic politics-based reasons, explaining the bias of political elites in favor of concentrating attention and resources on the privatization of state enterprises. For similar reasons, namely the large concentration of employment in failing privatized firms, the concentration on privatization "from above," also continued after 1997, that is during the period of macroeconomic restraint, reinforced by the weaknesses of transformation strategy with respect to the financial sector.

The story is repeated, for example, in Poland. Even now the privatization of badly performing, unprivatized heavy industry, as well as of the physical infrastructure sector (electricity, rail transport, etc.) generates great emotions and political battles. This is in spite of the fact that the private sector – new and privatized together – supplies more than 75 percent of aggregate GDP.

While stressing the limited attention accorded to the new private enterprises, in the Czech statistical records we have found only one microcensus, where the businesses (enterprises) were classified into two categories: old and new (*de novo*). The businesses included a large number of small firms, which were practically the only *de novo* firms under Czech indigenous ownership. The census covered the years 1990–96. The panel micro-data was based on the working history of 2,284 workers who worked from the 1980s until December 1996. Fortunately, the panel also described the firms where the workers had been employed earlier. But unfortunately no later extension of the project was undertaken (similar data gathering development we observed in Poland, see Chapter 5).

Jurajda and Terrell (2001) used the census in question for estimating the structure of firms that were classified into public sector (such as health service, education, and state administration), state-owned enterprises (SOEs), privatized SOEs, and *de novo* firms. By using the Monte Carlo method, they estimated the proportion of employment that belonged to each of these ownership categories. The estimated results are indicated in Figure 3.1.

The curve in Figure 3.1 depicting *de novo* firms shows that the process of privatization "from below" commenced in 1991 with their employment of approximately 8 percent of the total. Their size at that time was very small, in most cases equal to self-employment. The state sector was clearly

% of aggregate employment

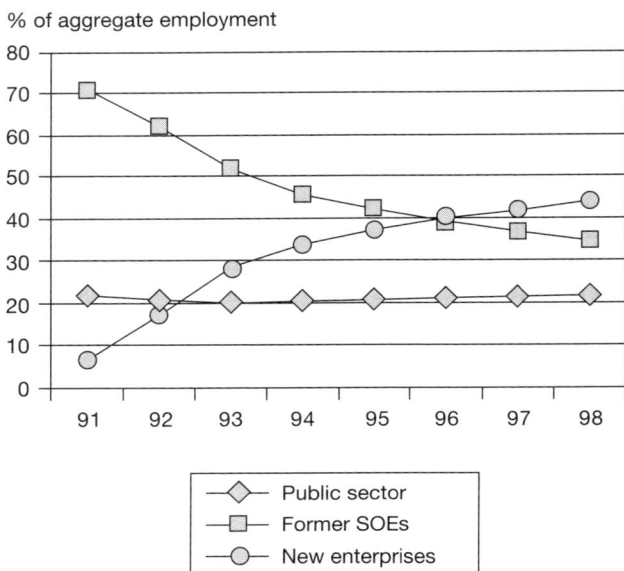

Figure 3.1 Changes in the composition of employment between old and new enterprises in 1991–1998.

Source: Jurajda and Terrell, 2001.

dominant, comprising the rest of the economy (privatization "from above" was still in the offing).

In spite of the initial small share, the dynamics of *de novo* firms in the early transformation period, 1991–93, was staggering. We can advance the hypothesis that the speed and the spontaneity of this process (at the end of 1993 over 30 percent of employees were working in the newly born firms) was one of the most valuable assets that Czech society produced in its quest for prosperity.

Although the build-up of new businesses slowed down after 1993, we estimate that by mid-1996 employment in *de novo* firms caught up with employment in former SOEs (at that time nearly all privatized by the so-called "mass privatization methods," primarily voucher privatization). The share of the SOE sector amounted to nearly 40 percent of the total. Afterwards, during the macroeconomic restraint and recession period (1997–99), and later during the relatively weak recovery, the growth of new indigenous businesses became rather erratic. Years of large increases in the number of SMEs alternated with those of small decreases. Data on the changing numbers of firms in the post-communist Czech Republic for the

Table 3.1 Number of firms in the Czech economy, 1991–1999 (in thousands)

Firms	1991	1993	1996	1998	1999
All registered firms	179	1,119	1,469	1,781	1,963
Self-employed	–	–	1,104	1,328	1,426
Juridical persons	54	133	231	297	343
SOEs	3.5	3.3	1.9	1.3	1.2
Public enterprises	–	–	16	15	15
Private firms and corporations	–	–	169	218	260
Sole proprietorships	–	–	1,238	1,484	1,620
Sectors and subsectors:					
Firms in agriculture	–	–	121	128	130
Firms in manufacturing	–	–	198	235	251
Firms in construction	–	–	158	187	209
Firms in trade	–	–	467	576	627

Source: *Statistical Bulletin*, Czech Statistical Office, Prague, 2000.

1991–99 period are shown in Table 3.1. The most recent data seem to confirm the pattern.

The dynamics of output growth has been greater in later years in the fast-growing foreign firms (primarily large MNEs). Nonetheless SMEs continued to be the prime area of employment growth (see, Jurajda and Terrell, 2001, from whom we reproduce Figure 3.1, above, as well as Benacek and Zemplinerova, 1997a, for earlier years).

Another statistical survey targeted on SMEs was made in 2001. Its size range was firms with the number of employees between 10 and 250. There, the distinction was made between *de novo* firms, privatized firms (acquisitions), and state-owned firms (see Mejstrik and Zemplinerova, 2001). We can estimate from the rather limited sample of 195 enterprises, selected from five industries, that in the year 2000 approximately 55–70 percent of all SMEs were established as "greenfield," that is *de novo*, firms and approximately 25–40 percent were acquisitions. Note however, that the "acquisitions" category is comprised both of old state enterprises, or their spun-off divisions, and of firms taken over by other firms, either new private or privatized. So, the share of *de novo* firms may have been somewhat higher.

Even more importantly, the sample excluded micro-enterprises employing nine persons or less. Thus, the actual share of new private firms in the national economy undoubtedly was *much* higher. As Table 3.2 indicates, there were large differences in these respects across industries. Unfortunately, these results were derived for firms with less than 250 employees only. It is certain that the extension of the sample to the remaining category of larger firms would decrease the average proportion of new firms in all firms. Then, it

Table 3.2 Distribution of new and old enterprises in a 2001 survey on SMEs (data for the year 2000)

Type of firm	Food	Clothing	Wood	Plastics	Information technologies	Total
New firms	(21) 54%	(33) 73%	(16) 67%	(15) 65%	(47) 73%	(132) 68%
Old firms	(16) 41%	(11) 24%	(7) 29%	(7) 30%	(16) 25%	(57) 29%
Total of all firms	(39) 20%	(45) 23%	(24) 12%	(23) 12%	(64) 33%	(195) 100%

Source: Mejstrik and Zemplinerova, 2001.

Note: The numbers in brackets represent the number of firms responding, the next number is the percentage of the given category in the given industry (or percentage of all responding firms in the last row).

The column totals do not tally exactly owing to the fact that a few firms could not be classified either way: for instance, where a new firm has been formed from a division of an old firm spun off in the process of privatization.

would make intuitively expected results compatible with the estimation of Jurajda and Terrell in Figure 3.1. That would also imply that the proportion of new firms in all firms with employment over 250 workers would have to be approximately as little as 25 percent, pointing to the rigidity in the sector of large firms.

The estimates from Table 3.2, plus extrapolated data from the previous studies of this author (Benacek, 1995 and 1997c) and the findings of Zemplinerova (2001) concerning productivity, may now be used to estimate the share of the authentic, entrepreneurial private sector in GDP. Our aim will be to estimate not so much the share of domestic *de novo* firms alone in GDP, but rather the share of a partly (or even largely) overlapping category of authentic private firms, characterized by stable ownership and management and aiming at strategic restructuring of production. That latter category will, therefore, include *de novo* indigenous private enterprises (e.g. "greenfield" domestic investments) and foreign acquisitions by strategic investors, who brought with them capital, new technologies, and competent management (i.e. a prospect of good corporate governance). Table 3.3 presents the respective data.

The problem with the Czech new private sector is that a large part of it is concentrated in very small (micro) firms that are very heterogeneous and on which the statistics are very scarce. Moreover, as also observed by Laky in Chapter 4 in the case of Hungary, an unknown share of the very small (self-employment) firms are tax avoidance ventures. Nevertheless, we have included them among the authentic private firms because they were founded as start-ups and no safe methodology of eliminating them from the population of firms is available. As to the medium-sized firms, we have estimated that

Table 3.3 Share of the authentic new private sector (domestic and foreign) in a given category of enterprises and in GDP in 2000

Enterprise category by size and type of ownership	Share of authentic private firms in total number of firms in a given category in %	Share of all firms in total output (value added). Aggregate output = 100%	Estimated share of authentic firms in total output (value added). Aggregate output = 100%
0–9 employees	95.0	11.0	10.5
10–250 employees	63.0	34.0	21.4
over 250 (foreign)	90.0	30.0	26.7
over 250 (indigenous)	15.0	25.0	3.8
All firms	X	1.00	**62.6**

Source: Own simulation based on estimates from the study by Zemplinerova (2001) and the data of the author.

more than a third of firms with 10–250 employees cannot qualify as new private firms because they were just separated and privatized divisions of former SOEs. And a large part of the successful firms in that medium-sized category are in fact foreign-owned enterprises.

The remaining indigenous firms in Table 3.3 are represented to a large extent by enterprises privatized by managers, other insiders, or management funds. These firms have been often heavily indebted, showing no signs of a successful restructuring. On the other hand, large firms under foreign ownership, with approximately 30 percent share of GDP, do not dominate the Czech economy (the way they do in Hungary).

Although the estimated 62.6 percent share of the aggregate authentic, entrepreneurial private sector in GDP is relatively high, we should realize that more than 37 percent of GDP still remains afflicted by the unresolved, or ill-defined property rights problems, failed restructuring, excessive debt, and general firm-level instability. It is in the foregoing sector of the economy that the market rules of the game are not fully enforceable. These firms can survive only in a conducive political environment, generating explicit or implicit subsidies. Inevitably, the afflicted sector affects adversely the performance of the healthy one. The former contributes in many ways to the aggregate budget deficit. First, explicit subsidies require budget expenditures. Second, the other debt forgiveness reduces revenues. Next, a large commercial debt of afflicted firms raises the cost of borrowing for healthy firms, and so on.

Thus, an increase in the economic growth rate depends also on restoring the economic health of the afflicted sector. An alternative is the perpetual reallocation of resources away from the economically healthy, but politically weak, sector to the politically important afflicted sector. The first meets political resistance; the second ensures reduced performance level and aggravating economic problems in the longer run.

Although the asymmetry between the conditions for expansion of *de novo* private firms and privatized SOEs (in favor of the latter) was apparent since the end of the first wave of voucher privatization in 1993, one cannot deny that SMEs were nonetheless gaining ground throughout the 1990s. In many respects the position of Czech SMEs in 1998 was comparable with that in developed industrial economies. According to CESTAT statistics (see Czech version of the bulletin, Czech Statistical Office, 2000) the ratio of registered entrepreneurs per 1,000 inhabitants (so-called entrepreneurial density) in 1998 was 139, while in Poland and Hungary the level was slightly more than a half of that (see Chapter 2). Even if the Czech statistics may have been biased (including tax-avoiding "forced" entrepreneurs), the intensity of private initiative in the Czech Republic in taking risks and running businesses was generally evaluated to be at the top among transition economies. Similarly Róna-Tas (1997) has estimated that Czech entrepreneurial activities have been among the most dynamic among the post-communist countries. Other statistics (see Szostkowski, 2003) show the Czech Republic's entrepreneurial density to be among the top three to four transition countries. Thus, at a minimum the Czech new private sector has been among the leaders in this respect.

Unfortunately, the comparative advantage stemming from the early entrepreneurial propensities of the Czech population was not reinforced by the well thought out regulatory regime and other public policy measures, enabling the new entrepreneurial firms to flourish. But politicians, caught between the alternatives of supporting the rapidly expanding new private sector or the ailing privatized or non-privatized SOEs, sided – as in other countries – with the latter. For the old privatized or non-privatized state sector had been both much more numerous at the start of transition (see above) and much better organized as a lobby.

Another question to be asked, while discussing the impact of new private firms, is how *de novo* firms affected the labor market. Munich *et al.* (1999) investigated how privatization "from above" and the emergence of *de novo* private firms changed the returns to human capital and how the new free wage setting modified the pre-transition narrow wage differentials in the state sector of the economy. The transition from the centrally planned to the market system resulted in a gradual increase in the rates of return to education, with the rates of return reaching West European levels by 1996.

This increase is found in all ownership categories of firms. For example, the return from a year of education was 5.6 percent in the state/public sector, 6.5 percent in privatized SOEs and 6.1 percent in the *de novo* private firms.

As to the returns of a year of experience, the difference was much more substantial. It was 1.5 percent in the state/public sector, 2.2 percent in privatized SOEs, and 3 percent in the *de novo* firms. There was another feature where *de novo* firms differed from the old firms. The wage policy differences are depicted in Figure 3.2. Although there was a general trend throughout the economy of increasing wages during the first 20 years of working experience, the increase was faster in *de novo* firms. But in the public and the privatized sectors wages did not decrease with age after 20 years of experience, in *de novo* firms there was observed a sharp decrease in wages for workers with more than 30 years of experience.

It seems that the newly established firms remunerated younger experienced workers particularly well relative to the older ones. Also, they paid higher wages to the recent entrants into the labor market than was the case in the privatized or public enterprises. Incidentally, this seems to be a more general pattern in post-communist transition. For example, similar conclusions are drawn in various studies on Poland and Hungary.

Comparative analysis of small and large firms

Due to the lack of detailed statistics on Czech *de novo* firms which we have already pointed out, we have taken the whole SME sector as a proxy in order to quantify their characteristics. Table 3.4 compares the size structure of SMEs in the Czech Republic with that in the European Union as a whole and in four different countries (two of them, Belgium and Austria, being EU members).

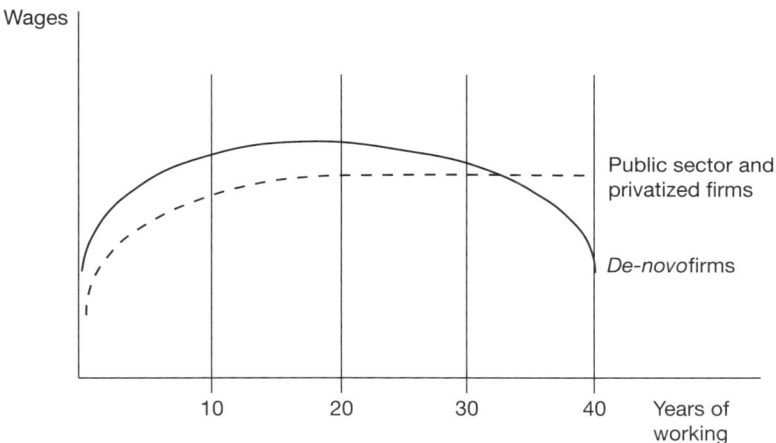

Figure 3.2 Varied wage policies in firms.

Table 3.4 Size distribution of firms: comparison of the Czech Republic and selected countries (plus the EU as a whole) in the 1990s

Country/Area	Number of enterprises Shares in total (in %)			Number of employees Shares in total (in %)			Value added Shares in total (in %)		
	1 – 99	100–499	500 +	0 – 99	100–499	500 +	0 – 99	100–499	500 +
USA	98.1	1.6	0.3	38.5	14.6	46.9	14.3	13.6	72.1
Japan	96.0	3.5	0.5	23.7	25.3	51.0	34.8	29.7	35.5
Belgium	98.9	0.9	0.2	45.4	19.5	35.1	54.4	18.6	27.0
Austria	86.1	12.1	1.8	40.6	36.0	23.4	27.4	36.4	36.2
Czech Republic	98.1	1.5	0.4	28.0	27.8	44.2	20.9	24.3	54.8
European Union	98.9	0.9	0.2	53.3	16.2	30.5	50.0	21.4	28.6

Source: OECD, Meeting of the Industry Committee – Scoreboard of Indicators, Paris, February 1998, p. 81 and the Czech Ministry of Industry, 2000. Data are for 1992, with the exception of USA (1993) and the Czech Republic (1998).

Under the communist economic system, i.e. until 1990, the size structure of Czech firms was dominated by large and very large firms; firms with fewer than 500 employees were scarce. The needs of the capitalist market economy dictated a radically different size structure. Taking into consideration historical roots (common rules of the game in the Hapsburg empire) and similarities in factor endowments, the size structure of Czech businesses should be expected to converge on the Austrian structure. Austria is a country with an exceptionally large number of medium-sized firms and with low value added per worker in small firms. In another words, Austrian small businesses (like, for example, those in the United States) are highly labor-intensive with low capital requirements.

This type of specialization would be advantageous for Czech small firms because they have had typical post-communist country difficulties with acquiring capital. This characteristic feature is in contrast with, e.g., that of SMEs in Belgium, where small firms are well endowed with capital and their value added per employee is therefore bigger than in large firms.

The tendency of SMEs to use labor more intensively than large firms was already apparent in the Czech economy in early transition. First, SMEs concentrated their activities to a large extent in labor intensive goods and services producing sectors (clothing, textiles, wood-processing, metal-working, glass, trade, personal services). Second, the overall allocation of resources in all industries (i.e. including the capital-intensive ones) favored more intensive labor usage that substituted for the expensive new physical capital. There are a few determinants of the described pattern:

a   Since transition means a new beginning in shaping the size structure of the economy, the lesson from the economics of development applies. With little capital, new firms start in these sectors and branches of the economy, where capital requirements are low. That means, first of all, in retail trade, but also in light industries, construction, and personal services. Usually capital accumulated there serves further expansion, which gradually spills over to more capital-intensive activities in the same branches and sectors, or to other more capital-intensive branches of the national economy;

b   Those SMEs (the large majority) which have been established as *de novo* firms had very little capital at the start. The story was different in the case of privatized firms or those divisions that were spun off from larger state firms. The latter "inherited" capital at zero or a heavily discounted price;

c   For the new private firms capital had to be acquired at the market. Although there was an excess supply of second-hand capital (buildings, machinery, and equipment), so that prices were low, entrepreneurs had to pay nonetheless more than the prices at which similar assets were transferred to the privatized SOEs.

d   Availability of credit lines to SMEs is traditionally restricted relative to those of large firms (for a theoretical rationale, see Luczka, 2001). But in early transition economies entrepreneurs suffered additionally from the non-existent track record of their earlier business performance and credit repayment;

e   And, in order to begin and end on a general note, relative wages between Czechs and employees in the EU countries suggested greater specialization in labor-intensive activities. Traditional prescriptions of the theory of comparative advantages applied also to the Czech economy.

The size structure in the EU economies – outside the German speaking area – is dominated by small firms. The Czech structure still has some distance to cover in order to close the gap to the average in the European Union. There still remains a gap to be filled by future expansion in either the medium-sized firms subsector (an increase of employment by 30 percent, to reach the level of Austria) or in the subsector of small firms (an increase of employment by 90 percent, to reach the average level of the EU). In either case, the expansion of SMEs must take place, as it has been the case so far, at the expense of the shrinking large firms sector.

At the same time the SME sector itself should be expected to change its structure. Although its share in the aggregate Czech employment is not much different from that in advanced countries, some note an over-employment in the subsector of very small firms (microenterprises and sole proprietorships). There are too many part-time jobs, sometimes in parallel with full-time employment in the state sector. Such firms are not very productive and they may even mask the existence of hidden unemployment.

Another aspect of the search for potential room for expansion of SMEs may be highlighted by comparing the present situation in the Czech economy with that of the Taiwanese one. Taiwan is an industrially advanced country with approximately $18,000 GNP per capita, whose development was overwhelmingly associated with SMEs. In 1998 the SME sector employed 78 percent of the domestic labor force. Taiwan is at one end of the continuum of the size structure of the economy; its SME sector is almost the largest among the middle to highly developed economies. Taiwanese SMEs function mainly as flexible providers of intermediate goods and services to large enterprises – their share in total final sales was only 31 percent. While the Belgian experience suggests capability of SMEs to absorb high capital intensity, the most important lesson from Taiwan is that SMEs are also able to absorb high R&D-based technology.

The jump-start of SMEs in East-Central Europe was one of the most important developments in post-communist transition. However, the development of SMEs has not so far reached either the Taiwanese sophistication in SME development, or the growth rate of the formation of new firms and output growth observed at various times there and in some other high-growth countries.

The only sector where SMEs recovered very quickly and actually expanded their share of employment and output was manufacturing. This is surprising, since it is precisely a slowdown in the business cycle which usually affects the manufacturing sector most strongly, and the recovery started only in mid-2000. After 1998 the position of large firms in manufacturing stabilized mainly due to intensive inflows of FDI. Thus, the performance of the large firms improved on the average, although they continued to shed employment (and many domestically owned large firms continued to suffer from the unfinished restructuring). Between 1995 and 2000 employment in firms with 500 employees and more decreased by almost one-third (32.4 percent). Thus, the pattern described in Chapter 2 also occurred in the Czech Republic.

The industrial sector, primarily manufacturing, stagnated in terms of total employment. What large firms lost was gained by small firms, but total, or aggregate, employment in 1995–98 increased only by 1.3 percent. A similar story in terms of relative shares of the small and large firms took place in a majority of sectors. More details are presented in Table 3.5. Small firms' share in total employment increased everywhere at the expense of large firms, except in construction and trade.

The dynamics of the SME sector first started to slow down after 1993. One reason for the slowdown is the very low starting point; the increases in absolute terms in the number of firms naturally could not go as fast after the first few years. The story was repeated in other countries, including Hungary

Table 3.5 Shares of SMEs in employment, sales value, and value added in the aggregate figures for each sector of the Czech economy, in 1995 and 2000 (in %)

Sector	Employment		Sales		Value added	
	1995	*2000*	*1995*	*2000*	*1995*	*2000*
Agriculture	73.4	85.7	75.1	83.4	76.0	81.6
Industrial sector	35.1	46.7	29.2	35.2	28.4	34.7
Construction	72.5	80.6	72.0	74.3	75.1	77.4
Trade	83.9	83.4	88.3	86.6	89.2	85.3
Transport	18.2	26.2	49.7	39.6	31.8	23.9
Other services	82.6	84.7	88.4	87.0	84.4	82.4
Total	54.6	61.3	63.6	62.6	53.9	53.7

Sources: SME database of CSO and estimates.

and Poland. But the rate of expansion of output of the already existing private firms might have other contributing factors. For example, the slow restructuring in the domestically owned corporate sector maintained the production factors (labor, capital) in inefficient large firms, which could not therefore be used in expanding SMEs. The latter could not outbid inefficient large firms in terms of wages and prices as non-restructured enterprises have been backed by soft fiscal policies, generous bank loans, and various bailout and "revitalization" schemes.

In Table 3.6 we compare labor productivities in SMEs and large enterprises in the years 1997 and 2000. One might have assumed that since new private firms are expected to be more adaptive and efficient, they should also display higher labor productivity. But with three exceptions for 1997, labor productivities across industries were lower than in large firms.

The simple comparison of labor productivities across the size structure is not, however, a methodologically proper approach. First and foremost, large firms generally use more capital-intensive technologies. In capital-intensive

Table 3.6 Value added per employee: comparison of SMEs and large firms, 1997–2000

	1997			2000		
Sector	*SME* *CZK '000*	*Large* *CZK '000*	*SME/* *Large* *(%)*	*SME* *CZK '000*	*Large* *CZK' 000*	*SME/* *Large* *(%)*
Coal mining	253	416	60.9	241	518	46.5
Other mining	436	185	235.9	489	516	94.8
Food	250	446	56.1	290	579	50.1
Textile and apparel	141	188	75.3	201	241	83.2
Leather	144	143	100.7	161	167	96.5
Wood products	210	257	81.4	226	411	55.0
Paper & publishing	337	392	86.1	365	826	44.2
Coke, ref. petroleum	–	1060	–	–	1959	–
Chemical products	455	556	81.7	669	770	87.0
Rubber and plastic	316	354	89.2	353	522	67.8
Mineral products	321	440	73.1	406	593	68.4
Metals	266	310	85.9	328	390	84.1
Machinery and eq.	278	243	114.1	312	325	96.0
Electr. & optical eq.	306	261	117.1	346	371	93.3
Transport equipment	285	427	66.6	374	573	65.3
Other manufacturing	191	232	82.5	238	326	73.0
Electricity, gas, w.	347	853	40.7	539	1191	45.3
All industry	261	376	69.3	317	522	60.8
All economy	263	335	78.5	337	435	77.4

Source: Czech Statistical Office, database of SMEs, 2002, own calculations.

industries the difference may be overwhelming; there, even the product structure is radically different. Where capital-poor SMEs, especially small firms, have an advantage is capital productivity. As they combine their abundant labor (in accordance with their comparative advantage) with their scarce capital assets, they obtain much larger output, sales, and value added per unit of capital. This latter advantage carries over in many industries to total factor productivity as well. It should be noted that in the specific circumstances of post-communist transition, SMEs still need not display lower labor productivity than the large domestic firms, as was found by Zemplinerova (2001). Given the slow restructuring and associated problems of privatized firms (see Chapter 2), SMEs may perform better for a number of years even with respect to indicators where normal, healthy large firms usually display a strong advantage. This becomes clear as we compare SMEs with indigenous privatized SOEs and not with the subsidiaries of multinational firms. In the industrial (secondary) sector approximately 40 percent of all large firms are firms established by means of FDI and their productivity is approximately 85 percent higher than that of indigenous firms of similar size. That would substantially narrow the gap in labor productivity of SMEs (from 60.8 percent to 81 percent of the average for the subset of large domestic enterprises in 2000). And, certainly, the profitability of small firms need not be lower than that of large firms, as is confirmed by scattered data from the very few countries for which there are some statistics available (see Hungary, Poland, and Estonia, in Szostkowski (2003)).

Job creation and job destruction in small and large firms

Czech SMEs have different factor proportions than the large corporate sector. The production of the former is more labor-intensive and the share of wages in value added increases as the size of the enterprise decreases. By contrast, for a variety of reasons, at the same time they proportionally invest less in physical assets. During the 1990–2000 period, the Czech authentic private sector (SMEs and foreign investment enterprises) were important net creators of jobs, while the privatized SOEs were constantly losing jobs (see Jurajda and Terrell, 2002). This is a development observed in all transition economies (see, for example, Bilsen and Konings, 1998, as well as McMillan and Woodruff, 2002). In order to test empirically the differences in employment behavior between SMEs and large enterprises, we designed the model explained in Figure 3.3.

The model describes a situation in an enterprise where production is a function of labor subject to constant returns, described by π_0. Product Q_0 is sold on a perfectly free market at price P_0. As the productivity increases, the

P – price

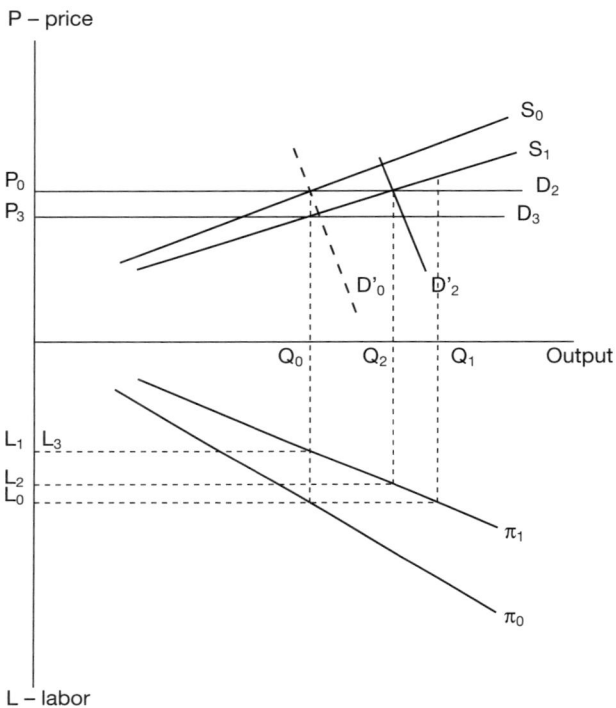

Figure 3.3 Interdependence between employment, productivity, supply, and demand.

production function shifts to π_1. In no case can employment remain at L_0 because production Q_1 has no demand. If the enterprise prefers to keep quantity unchanged (and internalize its ensuing rent into a higher profit), instead of decreasing the price sharply, subject to inelastic short-run demand D'_0, it will have to cut down on labor proportionally with its increase in productivity. Employment will have to be reduced to L_1.

However, as the medium-run demand curve (D_2) becomes perfectly elastic, the firm can sell Q_2, which requires raising employment to L_2. The last change can happen exogenously from the demand side. For example, if the exogenous prices fall from P_0 to P_3, then the long-term demand shifts from D_2 to D_3. Employment must be adjusted proportionally to the demand shock and be cut from L_2 to L_3.

Now we can study whether the real economy behaves in accordance with this simple model. The relevant variables are employment, sales, and productivity in the firm. In the ideal case we should also test unit prices, but this variable is not empirically available for enterprises. We can drop it from our tests, given the condition that medium-term prices are exogenous and demand is perfectly elastic. Thus, any price change is reflected in the value of sales ($P \times Q$), though this relationship is less than unity because even the short-run demand curve is not completely inelastic. The production (sales) values should be in constant prices, so that we can calculate more easily the volume of production (Q).

The model for testing will be:

$$L_i = a \times Q_i^{\ b} \times VA/L_i^{\ c} \times \varepsilon_i,$$

where L = employment, Q = output (sales), VA/L = productivity, ε = error term, $i = 1, 2, \ldots, 25$ sectors, $\{a, b, c\}$ = estimated coefficients.

It is assumed for the purpose of a hypothesis testing (according to our model) that coefficient c should be negative and equal to unity. Coefficient b should be positive, but its value is subject to more complicated relationships:

a   It depends on the way a change in labor productivity is transformed into a shift of the supply curve. If the share of labor (wages $\times$ L) in value added is low (i.e. the production is capital-intensive), than the reaction of the supply curve (like a shift of S_0 to S_1) is also small, which has an insignificant impact on employment.

b   If the demand curve is inelastic, any potential increase in Q (due to a gain in productivity) offers little opportunity for a supply expansion. Instead of creating new jobs there is a price fall.

c   If the elasticity of the production function is low, then even a sharp decline in unit costs generates a low response in terms of increased employment.

Coefficient b is expected to be higher for small firms than for corporations because their production is more labor-intensive, production function is more elastic, and demand curve is flatter (it should be perfectly elastic for price-takers).

The foregoing model was tested on Czech data for 1997–2000 (taking logarithms of all variables). The sectors covered 15 manufacturing industries, two mining sectors, agriculture, forestry and five service sectors. The estimation of coefficients produced the characteristics shown in Table 3.7.

As Table 3.7 shows, both tests are in line with our hypotheses, since all coefficients are highly significant and have the signs expected. SMEs reveal their tendency for high job creation during all four years tested, while the characteristics for large enterprises point to their job-shedding propensity,

Table 3.7 A: SMEs (up to 250 workers)

	Coefficient	Standard error	t-statistics	P-value
Intercept	4.164	0.3598	11.57	0.000
Production (sales)	1.050	0.0189	55.63	0.000
L-productivity	−0.823	0.0573	−14.36	0.000
	R-squared adj. = 0.969	SEE = 0.307		D–W = 2.09

Note: These enterprises had a 60 percent share in total employment in 2000.

B: Large enterprises (with more than 250 workers)

	Coefficient	Standard error	t-statistics	P-value
Intercept	6.971	0.4759	14.65	0.000
Production (sales)	0.964	0.0327	29.41	0.000
L-productivity	−1.139	0.0682	−16.68	0.000
	R-squared adj. = 0.907	SEE = 0.367		D–W = 1.58

Note: These enterprises had a 40 percent share in total employment in 2000.

even in those years when they were expected to stabilize and later grow. Job creation in SMEs was promoted from three factors:

a   Growing demand for their products;
b   Elasticity of employment relative to production (higher than unity);
c   Less than proportional reduction of employment due to productivity increase.

Large enterprises had all these three characteristics reversed. The surprisingly high negative elasticity of employment *vis-à-vis* productivity changes can be explained by a reversed causal relationship: in order to gain competitiveness, these firms had to restructure their production and downsize their employment, which was inherited from the communist times of persistently excess demand for labor (see Chapter 1).

As stressed in Chapter 2, increased productivity in large, privatized firms stemmed for a number of years from continuous labor-shedding, as the productivity levels per worker have been shifting upward toward Western standards. These processes have usually taken a long time, given the fact that 50 percent excess employment in communist enterprises had been a norm rather than an exception.

Main conclusions and policy implications

The main findings of the chapter can be summarized in the following manner:

- The lasting problems of Czech transition, which have been appearing at least since 1996, have their roots in the inefficient behavior of a significant part of the large domestic enterprise sector, that is the privatized SOEs. There, demand for the creation of authentic, self-reliant, well-performing firms gave way, under political pressure to "make haste slowly", to various forms of support, a transition equivalent of "soft" budget constraint under communism. Given the preponderant role of the non-privatized and later privatized SOEs in aggregate employment, the new entrepreneurial private sector has not been the policy priority throughout the transition period.

- This "soft" approach to the restructuring requirements of the SOE sector reinforced the inherited redistributive behavior at the level of firms. Unfortunately, as most transition countries, including the Czech Republic, learned the hard way, redistribution is from the more efficient to the less efficient, reducing the growth potential of the economy;

- The authentic, entrepreneurial private sector cannot be introduced "from above" as an act of social engineering, designed and implemented by bureaucratic hierarchies. It can emerge, get established and expand only through gradual steps taken one by one at the level of independent economic agents, making their decisions autonomously on factor and product markets. The grass roots initiative "from below" was what was required.

- Notwithstanding the lack of government support, intrusive regulations, arbitrary bureaucracy, and failing judiciary, the sector of new private firms has shown a high degree of viability and at the end of 1990s it became a dominant player on the market side of the Czech economy. It shows convincingly that the Smithian propensity to truck, barter, and generally make an effort to better one's lot is natural in human beings. If barriers to the improvement of their lot are not too high – and they certainly went down dramatically in the post-communist era – individuals and their private firms will do their utmost to overcome the still existing (or newly reestablished) barriers. This is what happened in the Czech Republic as well.

- As restructuring problems will diminish in size and urgency, we may hope that more time, effort, and resources will be spent on the institutional improvements which strongly benefit the new private sector. These entail deregulation, debureaucratization, reduced fiscalism and simultaneously reduced arbitrariness of the tax bureaucracy, and the strengthening of property rights enforcement. Every firm and every individual stand to gain therefrom, but smaller firms gain disproportionally more from less intrusive, low tax, and a more smoothly functioning institutional framework.

4 The Hungarian case

Mihaly Laki

Introduction

Privatization in a narrow sense is the transformation of state-owned assets (even whole companies) into privately owned ones. Privatization in a broader sense is measured by the growing share of the private sector in the national economy. The share of the private sector is increasing not only through the privatization in the narrow sense defined above, but also through the establishment and expansion of newly established, or *de novo*, firms (Kornai, 1992b). How important is the interaction between the two processes in the creation of a dominant private sector? Are the new private businesses the main source of economic dynamism and structural change in post-communist Hungary or are the privatized (previously state-owned) companies the engine of the economic recovery of the last years? This chapter is an attempt at an answer.

"Prehistory" of the issue

A small, but non-marginal, legally operating private sector existed in Hungary throughout the whole communist period. The intermittent periods of socialist reforms and reform reversals usually entailed changes in policies *vis-à-vis* the private sector. These, in turn, affected the political/economic framework, within which the private sector operated, both legally and illegally. Waves of intensified persecution or at least discrimination were superseded by waves of relaxation (Laki, 1999). In spite of the uncertainties generated by these ideological twists and turns, the legal private sector was able to survive even the worst periods.

Based on this interpretation we may reconstruct the institutional framework of and policies towards small private firms in the communist period. Institutions aimed at the rapid elimination of the remainder of the private sector had been established in 1949, when the "dictatorship of the proletariat" was (officially) declared, even if it had been in action since 1946. Voluntary associations of craftsmen (artisans) were at that time dissolved and new nation-wide ones, controlled from the top, were established.

Old and new associations differed sharply among themselves:

1   Membership was voluntary in the old and compulsory in the new associations.
2   Old-type associations were politically independent. Their representatives were elected by the members. The new ones were subordinated to the communist party. Their management was appointed by communist party *apparatchiki.*
3   Associations existing in the pre-communist period usually articulated and defended the interests of their members. The new creatures of the communist party were little more than a specialized subsystem within the central planning machinery. They transferred from top to bottom, that is to their members, the new, and ever-changing, rules of the game and output plan targets.

Little if anything was left of the private businesses' independence. Moreover, not only compulsory associations, but also other institutions of the planning system (tax offices, branch ministries) took part in regulating small businesses. The remaining small private firms were put at a largely permanent disadvantage *vis-à-vis* the state (or "socialized") sector.

The discrimination was most painful with respect to the following aspects of their operations:

•   Small private firm owners, as well as craftsmen, had to obtain special permits to buy a large (and ever-changing) number of production inputs;
•   Entry to and exit from local markets were restricted as well. Small private firms were excluded, for example, from markets in other towns than their own;
•   Small private firms were deprived of their most natural opportunities, that is of becoming subcontractors of state-owned firms; and
•   Small businesses were also usually victims of discriminatory pricing, that is they paid more than state-owned firms for the same material inputs or services.

At times not only were the rules of economic game skewed against them, but so were the general rules concerning personal freedom and property. There were earlier periods when brutal physical intimidation of private businessmen (especially peasants) served the main political/economic goals of collectivization. Other, non-economic areas of discrimination existed as well. Private entrepreneurs were excluded from the general pension and health care systems. Children of private entrepreneurs were discriminated against with respect to admission to secondary schools and universities.

These early severely discriminatory developments were gradually modified during the phases of economic reforms. Licensing of input procurement and prohibition of subcontracting to large state firms were abolished as early as the late 1950s. Entry into other than their own local markets by small private businesses was liberalized a few years later. The discrimination children from private sector against families with respect to school admission was abolished in 1962–63. Discriminatory pricing was in a large part eliminated by the system-wide reform of 1968.

Although the "residue of reforms" (Seleny, 1991), in spite of some setbacks, increased over the decades, the rules were liberalized to a only certain extent. Size limits (measured by a number of employees) never changed. The communist party-controlled institutional structure supervising and regulating the private sector was never disbanded. Associations continued to be controlled by the respective levels of the communist party apparatus and managed by the appointed *nomenklatura* till the very collapse of the communist system.

As signaled already, nothing was stable and lasting in the situation of the private sector. Throughout the period there never was any guarantee that the liberalization of constraints imposed on the private sector would not be suddenly reversed at some point. There were numerous cases, during periods of reform reversal, when old discriminative rules were re-imposed and new restrictions added.

However, in spite of all the discrimination, the legal private sector served as a prep school for thousands of entrepreneurs in the post-communist era. On the other hand, the economic dynamism of these people was severely constrained in the communist period (Róna-Tas, 1997). A distinctly small minority of the labor force worked for legal, registered private firms (see Table 4.1). The contribution of this sector to GDP was marginal as well (3.5 percent in 1989).

The *illegal* private sector produced much more than did the legal sector in socialist Hungary. The "official" estimate from the early 1980s – based on the calculations of the Central Statistical Office – was 16–19 percent of the national income (Lackó, 1992). Researchers came to similar conclusions (for example, Sik, 1987). Participating in a research project led by János Kornai, Mária Lackó extended the period of investigation to the last two to three years of the socialist system. Based on her monetary model she estimated that the share of the gray economy in GDP increased very fast and "it was 26 percent in 1988, 31 percent in 1989 and 34 percent in 1990" (Lackó, 1992: 161).

The strikingly large aggregate value of the gray economy resulted from putting together the widespread supply of unregistered services, unregistered

Table 4.1 Individuals and registered firms active in the legal private sector in 1989

Branch	Number of	
	Individuals	*Firms*
Craftsmen and merchants		
Craftsmen (in industry, construction and services) working full time	–	174,837
Craftsmen working part time (having a job in the state sector)	–	54,446
Tradesmen in retail trade	–	39,612
Others		
Owners of household plots and collective farmers' auxiliary plots	1,435,000	–
Members of economic partnerships in state-owned firms	184,000	–
Memorandum item		
Economically active population (in 1987	4,822,700	–

Source: Statistical Yearbook of Hungary, 1987 and 1990.

urban and rural construction activities, agricultural production for own consumption (and partly for sale to town dwellers), etc.

How may we explain the very limited contribution of hundreds of thousands of small businesses to GDP? Why did so many produce so little – between 3 percent and 4 percent of GDP (see, again, Table 4.1)? There is a number of explanations available. We have to take into consideration that for the most part private firms were what we call nowadays *micro-enterprises*. More often than not they were one-person operations. Besides, they functioned with very little physical capital. As stressed in Chapter 2, when the level of risk is very high, the time horizon of a business firm is shortened drastically. Therefore, the propensity to invest was very low in the legal private sector. In agriculture the household plots were tiny; on the average such a plot was equal to 0.76 hectare in 1989. Besides, a large majority of them spent only a part of their working time in their private ventures because they were employed in the state sector (Laki, 1994).

No wonder, then, that a large part of these low-productivity ventures disappeared with the beginning of post-communist transition. There was strong demand for the private sector, but not necessarily in the legal/ organizational forms that fitted best the shortage economy. Many ventures, such as economic partnerships and registered private firms, were dependent on symbiotic (and at times even parasitic) relationships with the large state-owned firms or semi-nationalized cooperatives. With the output decline of the state enterprises, economic partnerships in industry, for example, declined by almost half (from 6,125 to 3,623) between 1989 and 1994. To give another example of low productivity arrangements, household plots covered 281,000 hectares in 1989 and only 37,000 hectares four years later. Similar developments were observed elsewhere as well.

We have no good statistics about the migrations of those who worked for these and other "organizational hybrids of socialism." Nonetheless a series of more than 100 of in-depth interviews conducted between 1995 and 1999 suggests that a majority of these entrepreneurs changed the *legal form* of doing business and established firms which fitted better into the new market environment.

Apart from legal reorganization, the fall of communism opened up new vistas for the expansion of the private sector. Not only did the activities pursued under communism by the private sector, which had until then been persistently constrained, become open to legally and politically unconstrained expansion, but a whole array of *new* production and service activities was also thrown open to private entrepreneurship. However, many of these activities certainly required different types of skills than those in agriculture, retail trade, and manufacturing.

We assume, following Eric Jones (1988), and going back to the fountainhead, i.e. Adam Smith, that striving to better one's lot is a lasting feature of humanity. For the most part of human history it has been, however, severely constrained by the existing rules of the game and by the policies applied within those rules. Therefore, while moving from the "prehistory" to the history of the new private sector, I am going to devote a substantial part of this inquiry to various types of government-initiated developments. Privatization, deregulation, and support for the emerging private business sector will be given special attention. More general issues of liberty, law and order, and social capital are dealt with in Chapter 2.

Privatization

Every Hungarian government in the post-communist period, regardless of its ideological color, has signaled to the general public that the emerging market economy would be dominated by the private ownership of productive assets. The credibility of that message depended (among other factors) on the speed and transparency of privatization. But the room for maneuver of each post-communist government (with respect to the regulatory framework, and the mix of privatization methods) was continuously influenced by macroeconomic requirements of the national economy. This was especially true with respect to the growing budget deficit and foreign debt of the country in the 1991–95 period.

The worsening macroeconomic position of the country in the first years of the post-communist transition (see Table 4.2) helps us to understand why the direct sale method dominated the change in ownership structure of the former state sector. The financial requirements of the Treasury had a priority over other privatization goals and adversely affected the prospects of potential *Hungarian* buyers, who participated only occasionally in larger privatization projects (Giday, 1998).

Budgetary requirements explain also why the so-called voucher, or citizens' privatization, which by its very nature is unable to produce budgetary revenues, was excluded from the range of methods applied in Hungary. The "mainstream" Hungarian experts, including academics, opposed the introduction of that method, but their argumentation played, in my opinion, a secondary role only.

Moreover, the story of restitution, or the return of property to former owners, clearly showed the impact of macroeconomic stability requirements upon the choice of methods of privatization. In spite of the strong preferences for restitution within the then ruling political coalition, Treasury financial requirements limited not only the number of people entitled to restitution, but also the level of compensation, or restitution in kind, they were entitled to (Comisso, 1995).

There may have been other forces at work, though. A well-known survey (see Winiecki, 1992) revealed that among the seven countries surveyed Hungarians showed little enthusiasm for restitution, giving much stronger

Table 4.2 Some macroeconomic stability indicators for Hungary, 1989–1999

Year	Net foreign debt (Mill. US$)	Balance of payment in % of GDP	Net foreign debt in % of GDP	Budget of central govt. (in % of GDP)
1989	14,900	–	–	–
1990	15,936	–	–	–
1991	14,554	–	–	0.4
1992	13,052	–	35.6	–2.2
1993	14,927	–9.0	38.7	–5.5
1994	18,935	–9.4	44.3	–6.8
1995	16,817	–5.6	36.1	–8.2
1996	14,655	–3.7	32.4	–6.5
1997	11,805	–2.1	25.8	–3.5
1998	12,877	–4.9	27.4	–
1999	11,312	–4.3	23.3	–
2000	12,236	–3.3	24.7	–
2001	11,796	–	–	–

Source: Statistical Yearbook of Hungary, 2001.

support to sale to the highest bidder. Thus, social preferences coincided with Treasury financial requirements.

The emergence of the new, expanding entrepreneurial stratum and the ability of new owners' to survive in the very turbulent economic environment of early transition were strongly influenced by these circumstances. It should also be added that the accumulated savings of Hungarians were very limited (as in other post-communist societies). Moreover, again as everywhere, new small businesses (individual proprietors and smaller limited liability companies) were in a more difficult financial position than larger players in the market game. The reasons were either related to the transition itself, that is the lack of a track record of earlier borrowing or insufficient collateral, or were more general, such as higher risk of lending to small firms (see Luczka, 2001). Consequently, they faced a serious barrier in acquiring the financial resources needed to participate in privatization projects.

As everywhere, in Hungary too, complaints were heard about discrimination the small business sector (see Ványai, 1995). This issue was considered in general terms in Chapter 2. Here it is worth noting that other, more positive, assessments exist as well (see Bratkowski *et al.* 1991). They tend to show a more benign picture of the SME–financial sector interaction in transition.

But apart from the usual problems of financing business expansion, the typically more difficult access of small and medium-sized firms to borrowing also had marked consequences for the pattern of Hungarian privatization. The difficulties in obtaining loans to allow entrepreneurs to buy state-owned assets made it difficult to benefit from the privatization of larger or middle-sized state enterprises. The most entrepreneurs could usually do with their own and family savings, as well as with their firms' profits, was to take part in occasional sales by the State Property Agency (SPA) of some second-hand equipment or real estate. Managers of state-owned companies had greater opportunities to participate in privatization projects (Boda and Neumann, 1998), because given their *nomenklatura* connections they could get relatively large loans from the still state-owned (and *nomenklatura*-managed) banks. Nonetheless the outright sale method favored financially strong investors and that meant *foreign* investors first and foremost. This is the main reason why the majority of privatization revenues of the SPA came from foreigners (see Table 4.3).

Post-communist deregulation

Business entry decisions and owners' strategies (and, therefore, also the number of newly established private firms) were strongly influenced by the reality of transition. Both the recognition of systemic change and the accumulation of everyday experience by business people and potential

Table 4.3 Privatization revenues: share of receipts from foreign investors in the total revenues of central government

Year	Share of foreign revenues (in %)
1990	79.1
1991	80.9
1992	61.2
1993	67.3
1994	7.4
1995	87.2
1996	57.0
1997	61.1
1998	37.0
1999	61.0
1990–99 (weighted average)	62.7

Source: Mihályi, 2000: 867.

entrants that the persistent discrimination of the private sector has indeed come to an end affected the decisions in question. The political programs of the most influential political parties all strongly supported the idea of a market economy dominated by the private sector (Laki, 2000).

This resulted in a series of measures that transformed the rules of the game. Deregulation, understood at the threshold of the new economic system as the eradication of any discrimination against the private sector, and strong legal guaranties created by the new legislation establishing the market order, sent a strong positive signal. It indicated that the private property-based market economy was there to stay.

Thus, the modified old Hungarian Constitution established the equal status of state and private property. Other important acts passed by the first freely elected parliament, or by the executive, separated the economy from politics. Political parties were banned from organizing local units in business firms and public administration, including that of local governments (something very obvious in the West, but a welcome novelty in post-communist countries). The restrictions on the size of private enterprises (the upper limit on the number of employees, for example) and the prohibition of private activities in various areas of the Hungarian economy (banking, insurance, foreign trade) were abolished as well. There are no barriers any more to establishing local or national associations, or to articulating and/or defending the interests of private entrepreneurs.

These issues were of crucial importance for entrepreneurs. In 58 of the 97 interviews made by this author with owners-managers of SMEs mentioned earlier, they pointed to the new political order and the abolition of systematic discrimination against private business as important factors in their decision to start a private firm. The results of this non-representative sample survey, covering the 1989–92 period, are positively correlated with those of a larger survey made by György Lengyel. The latter survey points to the significant increase in the entrepreneurial proclivity of Hungarians in the first years of the post-communist transition.

"In 1988 one-fourth of the Hungarian adult population showed entrepreneurial proclivity," wrote Lengyel, "and in 1990 it was found that entrepreneurial proclivity rose to 44 percent. Two years later that indicator decreased to 27 percent" (Lengyel, 1997–98: 38). The survey indicates the temporary but strong effect of political change and the resultant new business climate.

The organizational support framework for the SME sector and its peculiarities

Economic philosophy and organization of support

The first, conservative Hungarian government perceived the existence of an imbalance between the strong position of large foreign firms and the weak position of small Hungarian firms. Therefrom stemmed a series of (weakly coordinated) attempts to elaborate effective policies and create a network of organizations supporting the small business. The perception of the need for an activist governmental approach to SMEs has been at the roots of every successive regulation and policy measure since 1989. Although there have been continuous organizational rearrangements, there is always one body or another which serves as the coordinator of interaction between the government and the small and medium-sized firms and their association.

It is a meeting place of bureaucrats from those ministries whose regulatory and other activities have an impact upon governmental policy towards the SMEs, representatives of business associations, and individual members of the business community (invited in a personal capacity by the Minister of Economic Affairs). The main task of this body is to improve the level of communication between business and government and to formulate consensus statements on strategic issues (A kis és középvállalkozás, 1997).

The interaction between the regulators on the one hand and the regulated on the other has also been established at the *local* level. Local governments in larger towns established their own organizations of small business support. In smaller towns or villages local governments employ specialists responsible for these activities.

There are several private profit-making or non-profit organizations whose aim is to contribute to the development of SMEs. The Hungarian Business

Development Fund is the principal organization of small business support in the non-agricultural sector of the economy. It was established in 1990 as an independent institution, with the start-up capital supplied then by parliamentary appropriation (4.2 bill. HUF). It's purpose is to assist the expansion of existing private firms employing less than 150 persons or registering a turnover of less than 300 mill. HUF per year, as well as to contribute the start-up capital for newly established enterprises. The main forms of support have been preferential loans, guaranties, and subsidies. The Fund established a nationwide network of local business centers and advisory offices. These centers formulate local support programs or evaluate individual projects. They also administer training programs. The centers operate on a non-profit basis. Local governments, business associations, and banks additionally contribute to their expenses, but the main sources of their budget financing are the contributions of the Hungarian Business Development Fund and the PHARE program. The centers offer a number of different preferential loans. The so-called Reorg/Start loan is available only for micro businesses employing no more than three persons. PHARE program loans are available for small and medium-sized companies, in which the share of Hungarian state or that of a foreign investor is less than 50 percent.

Different programs of the Ministry of Labor, which aims at maintaining jobs, are also offered on very favorable conditions to small businesses. Agriculture has its own system of small business support. There are more than ten different types of preferential loans available for agricultural small businesses.

One of the disadvantages of the small business is the difficulty of access to bank lending (see above, in this chapter, as well as Chapter 2. See also Luczka, 2001). Consequently, the Hungarian government established a mechanism of loan guarantees and interest rate subsidies. The Ministry of Finance, Ministry of Industry, Tourism and Trade, and Ministry of Agriculture all have their own mechanisms of support. The size of supported enterprises differs across projects, but the ceiling is the same everywhere; companies employing more than 500 persons are excluded from these schemes.

The government has also established a Loan Guaranties Company. The aim of the company is to help the banks in lending to non-agricultural firms, employing no more than 300 persons. The Guaranty Fund of Agrobusiness has the same purpose.

So far I have stressed various governmental initiatives. These initiatives are supported at the central and local levels by business associations, mostly new, established after the systemic change, but also in the few reestablished ones. However, in spite of their more or less active involvement in the support programs for the SMEs, their membership continues to be very low (Czakó-Vajda, 1993). There are varying explanations of the phenomenon. One is the distrust in institutions which are statutorily expected to represent their members, because of the remembrance of the communist past. Then, statutorily independent institutions were little more than the transmission belt of the totalitarian regime and an instrument of control. However, trade unions have not shared that fate to the same extent.

Therefore, other hypotheses are also worth considering. For instance, another hypothesis is that the limited interest of business people in membership in such associations reflects the limited importance of the associations themselves. Since everybody takes care of the SMEs, with the government in the lead, why be active in organizations that contribute little value added, either in policy recommendation or policy implementation capacity?

Finally, we cannot reject a further hypothesis. Namely, that entrepreneurs, owners of small firms, concentrate on the survival of their businesses. With that myopic perspective they see few benefits in organizations which are offer them the realization of their common long-term goals, rather than the most pressing individual short-term goals. Given this interpretation low membership in business associations is a temporary phenomenon. As entrepreneurs, or a majority of them, mature and strengthen the position of their firms on the one hand, and associations begin to concern themselves with the more immediate problems of SMEs on the other, the role of business organizations may increase.

Policies and their effects

No detailed evaluations of the efficiency of small business support policies pursued by the successive post-communist Hungarian governments are available (apart from laudations from foreign analysts believing in the strong guiding hand of the state (see, for example, Bukhvald and Vilenski, 2003)). Cost/benefit analysis of particular programs or individual projects is also absent. For that reason we have to resort to *indirect* indicators. Occasional surveys yield some interesting information with respect to small businesses' interactions with their institutional environment.

Thus, an early survey made by Hungarian Business Development Fund showed that only 11 percent of small businesses were in (some form of) contact with their local centers and offices (Czakó and Vajda, 1993). The numbers of those who actually *benefited* from various services offered is smaller still. Based on the calculations of Teréz Laky, it had been revealed that in the first four years only about 7,000 small businesses, out of more than 900,000, obtained preferential loans (Laky, 1994).

Another program which helped the unemployed to start a business firm affected about 20,000 individuals (in the same period). A program aimed at saving workplaces threatened by restructuring or bankruptcy, managed by the National Employment Fund, accepted proposals of 389 applicant entrepreneurs in the 1992–94 period, mainly from small and medium-sized enterprises. These SMEs promised to maintain about 35,000 workplaces that otherwise were slated to be eliminated by the owners (Neumann, 1996).

The number of small businesses exceeded more than one million in 1995. Given that fact, the supporting activity of state authorities and state-funded organizations, such as HBDF, seems to have played a rather minor role in the structural changes that the Hungarian economy underwent in the period of post-communist transformation. And it is worth stressing that so far we have used only quantitative indicators of *participation*. We have said nothing about the *economic outcomes*. But there are no studies evaluating such outcomes, either. Therefore, we have to rely on what we know about comparable efforts undertaken elsewhere.

To begin with the program mentioned last, the experience with job creation or job-saving programs is generally negative. For every 100 jobs created, 60 to 90 jobs are lost. Subsidized employees simply crowd out non-subsidized employees with the similar level of skills and experience (for the case of Sweden, see Peter Stein, 2001). Similar stories are known with respect to job-saving programs. It is usually those entrepreneurs or managers who calculate that they are in any case able to survive that apply for job-saving subsidies. Otherwise, if they were to go under, they would be burdened, apart from other problems, with the repayment of the total or a prescribed part of the subsidy.

Preferential loans create efficiency problems of a different order. As pointed out by Joshua Charap (1993), "it is easier . . . to throw money at the problem than to try to address and understand the problem." It is not true, Charap underlines, that "bankers are bad without really trying to understand what their job is. Their job is to *select* projects, that is to accept more profitable and reject less profitable projects." And, let us add, to take into account the corresponding level of risk.

There may have been a period in Hungary (and elsewhere) when those dealing with the small business sector were not professional enough, given the lack of experience in dealing with SMEs. At that time some special programs, compensating for that disadvantage, made sense, although even then subsidized lending need not have been the best answer to the problem. Why? Because for every subsidized loan there is a corresponding tax to finance the subsidy.

"Is it appropriate to tax the more successful business to subsidize the less successful business?" asks Charap, and he answers in the negative. Thus, even if the loans to microenterprises or other SMEs might have helped the borrowers, it is not at all sure that the losses of potential revenue of other SMEs that grew more slowly or stagnated due to insufficient funds for expansion (resulting from higher taxes) might have exceeded the gains. And, since the general impact of *any* redistribution upon efficiency is usually adverse, the probability of such an aggregate outcome is quite high.

Evolution of the Hungarian new private sector

If we take into account the foregoing limitations on what the government can realistically do to make the business environment more conducive for the expansion of the private sector, it is worth inquiring what the main consequences of state intervention have been. What kind of changes have been induced by privatization, deregulation, and small business support programs? To start with, we should distinguish more narrowly defined consequences for the Hungarian business community and, next, turn to the broader consequences for the structure of the whole post-communist economy.

The most important have been consequences of what the people rightly perceived as the fundamental systemic change. It was the perception – stressed already – of the end of all politically motivated discrimination against the private sector and the constitutional guaranties of economic freedom. Both resulted from the change in the *political* system that generated the unprecedented expansion of the entrepreneurial private sector. And it is worth keeping in mind that this rapid growth took place in the face of the very deep "transformational recession," as Janos Kornai called the steep output fall at the start of the systemic change.

The number of private business units grew extremely fast in the first years of post-communist transition in Hungary (Table 4.4). By the end of the first decade of transition (1999) there were more than 1 million business firms in Hungary and two years later more than 1.1 million firms. As the population of the country is about 10 million, it suggests that every tenth Hungarian is a registered private entrepreneur (Sántha, 1996).

Given the realities of post-communist transition, however, we should make some important corrections to the picture that we have presented of the buoyant expansion of entrepreneurship. Dynamic as the expansion of entrepreneurship indeed was, not all forms of entrepreneurship would be comparable with those in the established market economies of the West. A substantial number of small businesses were little more than social security tax-avoidance operations, a phenomenon also known from some other countries in transition (see here, Chapter 3 on the Czech Republic and Chapter 5 on Poland).

The tax system loopholes allowed owner-managers of some larger or medium-sized private companies to force upon their employees the change in their legal status. Instead of continuing to work as employees, they were

Table 4.4 Expansion of business firms: most popular forms of ownership

	Limited liability companies		Individual proprietorships	
	Number	Previous year = 100	Number	Previous year = 100
1989	17,341		320,619	
1990	26,807	154.6	393,450	122.7
1991	43,439	268.0	510,459	129.7
1992	60,762	164.0	608,207	119.1
1993	86,867	142.9	715,105	117.6
1994	121,128	139.4	778,026	108.8
1995	106,245	87.7	791,496	101.7
1996	125,940	1,18.5	745,247	94.2
1997	147,388	1,17.0	659,690	88.5
1998	162,588	1,10.3	648,701	98.3
1999	165,307	101.7	660,139	101.7
2000	171,495	103.9	682,925	103.3
2001	177,424	103.4	698,001	102.1

Source: Statistical Yearbook of Hungary, 2001.

asked to become subcontractors. Working at the same workplace, with unchanged technical conditions, they were offered supply contracts with the company as licensed entrepreneurs. Such "forced entrepreneurship" arrangements artificially boost the number of firms. Incidentally, as the three countries in question remain high income tax economies the phenomenon is bound to spread.

Apart from such social security tax avoidance operations, a number of firms were also boosted by purely criminal-type ventures. Various fly-by-night operators emerged and disappeared after a successful swindle (or a string of swindles). The only thing that was left was a firm in the register, and accordingly in the statistics. However, most of the difference between the number of active firms and that of registered firms stemmed from more prosaic – and lawful – causes.

Many individuals decided to obtain the license, swept by the wave of optimism resulting from the end of communist discrimination and the establishment of the principle of economic freedom. Having done that, they found they had no good idea as to what to do with their sudden entrepreneurial freedom, or were discouraged by difficult economic conditions.

The active registered firms, those which produce something and pay taxes, have been less numerous than registered firms by some 20–30 percent. Although substantial, this difference has not varied remarkably from those in other successful transition countries. In Poland, for example, that difference was slightly higher still, although slowly declining to about 30 percent by the late 1990s (see Chapter 5).

Therefore, even allowing for the active/non-active differential, the level of entrepreneurship has risen significantly in Hungary in the last dozen years. If we subtract the said 20–30 percent, the number of active private firms has still increased since 1989 by hundreds of thousands (compare data in Table 4.1 with those in Tables 4.4 and 4.5).

Moving from quantity to quality of policies, the newly founded firms have started – and remained – very small. Their smallness is not, we posit, completely independent of the above-mentioned barriers and weaknesses of Hungarian transition and the relative inefficiency of supporting measures. The number of the active individual proprietorships was 467,500 in 1999 and 99.6 percent of them employed ten persons or less. Another group of economic organizations, classified in the statistics as "limited liability companies and partnerships, total" (including joint stock companies, limited liability companies, limited partnerships, and cooperatives) is also dominated by small companies. The share of enterprises employing less than ten persons was 92 percent in 2001 (see Table 4.5).

The number of start-ups was extremely high in a number of industries and other sectors of the economy that had been dominated previously by large companies. New private firms soon began to dominate such sectors as agriculture, textiles, clothing, furniture, etc. The rapid expansion of the new private sector, first in terms of the number of firms and, later, of output has significantly contributed to the change in the ownership structure of the national economy.

The share of the state sector has diminished very fast since 1990. At the beginning of the second decade of transition the Hungarian economy is dominated by the private sector. Moreover, the established preferences for the

Table 4.5 Limited liability companies and partnerships differentiated by size in 2001

Number of employees	Number of firms	%
500 or more	472	0.13
250–499	597	0.16
50–249	4,918	1.32
20–49	8,795	2.36
10–19	12,855	3.84
1–9	186,604	50.19
0 or unknown	144,727	42.12
Total	334,702	100.00

Source: Statistical Yearbook of Hungary, 2001.

direct sale of SOEs to strategic investors have powerfully influenced the share of foreign investors in the aggregate share of private sector in the economy, as well as in the aggregate economy. That share became dominant in industry, banking, and insurance, and sizable elsewhere, except agriculture. Foreign-owned companies own nearly 60 percent of the total subscribed capital by 2000 (see Table 4.6).

In terms of size, the largest among the top five companies is the state-owned oil company, Mol Lt., but the next four firms are foreign-owned: Audi Hungaria, IBM Storage Products, Philips Group, and the formerly state-owned telecom, Matav, (Figyelõ, 2000). Almost three-quarters of the 200 largest companies registered in Hungary were wholly or partly owned by foreign investors 1997 (Diczházi 1998). There is no reason to expect that the pattern has changed since then.

The pattern in which foreign firms dominate the sector of large enterprises has been repeated in nearly all cases of successful transition countries. Since voluntary saving by the population has been strikingly low everywhere (in comparison with non-communist countries at similar development levels), the privatization of large SOEs made the foreign firms almost the only buyers of larger state firms. As a result, the ownership pattern of the large enterprise sector shows the domination of foreign firms and state-owned firms, either not yet privatized or not intended to be privatized. Fast-growing new private firms continue to be a minority in the large enterprise sector, although in successful countries it is a growing minority.

The new private sector dominates, on the other hand, the SME sector. The new private sector is composed of predominantly Hungarian firms, even if there is a large number of foreign-owned small and medium-sized firms (see

Table 4.6 Ownership structure of subscribed capital (enterprise applying double and single book-keeping rules) in 1992–1999 in percent

Year	Dominant owner(s') nationality Hungarian			Foreign	Other
	State	Private (indiv.)	Private (comp.)		
1992	52.1	10.2	0.0	11.4	26.2
1994	44.5	10.7	17.6	17.8	9.5
1995	25.7	11.5	19.1	26.8	17.0
1997	13.5	10.5	22.6	35.0	18.4
1998	12.0	10.7	25.6	40.3	11.3
1999	9.2	9.1	20.6	51.6	9.5
2000	7.2	9.2	18.0	58.5	6.4

Source: A kis és középvállalatok helyzete, 2000: 57–58.

Table 4.7 Shares of enterprises with Foreign Direct Investment involved by size categories of capital

Capital paid-in (mill. HUF)	Number of firms 1990	2001*
<1	2,019	6,634
1.1–10	2,453	13,982
10.1–50	696	2,565
50.1–100	178	811
100.1>	347	1,973
Total	5,693	25,365

Source: Statistical Yearbook of Hungary, 1999.

*Since 1997, without offshore enterprises and enterprises in which the share of FDI is under 10 percent.

Table 4.7). Numerically speaking, four foreign firms out of five are small or medium-sized ones.

Again the story is not unique, as in the Czech Republic and even more in Poland patterns have been very similar. An interesting feature of the growth pattern of small and medium-sized foreign-owned firms is that the share of non-growing firms in the aggregate is no different from the same share among Hungarian SMEs. A tentative conclusion may be drawn therefrom, although requiring further empirical inquiry, that "foreignness" (that is, the fact that the firm is foreign-owned) does not increase *per se* the probability of expansion in the SME sector.

How well did the *de novo* private sector perform?

Preliminary considerations

In this section we inquire into an issue not well researched empirically. Namely, into the existence, or non-existence, of the differentiated performance of two groups of companies: the newly established (*de novo*) firms registered as private after the collapse of communism, and former state-owned firms (SOEs) that have been transformed into private firms. A strand of thinking (see, first of all, Chapter 2 here, as well as Winiecki (2000b)) assumes that better initial assignment of property rights and a differential organizational/cultural heritage may determine the level of performance in the short to medium run in the post-communist economy. Unfortunately, there are no systematic statistical data available in Hungary on the sector of *de novo* firms. Therefore, we are unable to compare these firms directly with the group of privatized former SOEs.

As a second-best empirical choice, then, we compare two enterprise groups: large firms and small and medium-sized firms. The group of large companies consists of the majority of the already privatized or not-yet-privatized large SOEs. By contrast the large majority of micro, small, and medium-sized companies was registered *after* the collapse of communism.

We have, however, one more issue to deal with. While comparing the generic private sector (the one that was private from scratch) with the privatized one, we put together into one category the new private sector (established after the fall of communism) and the old private sector, that is private firms established before 1990. The distribution of both sub-categories of the entrepreneurial private sector can be established, making some rough approximations,

Dubious performance of pioneers

Applying the *content analysis* methodology, we have reconstructed the history of 23 companies established in the last years before the communist collapse by entrepreneurs who could be called the "pioneers" of capitalism. We use the term pioneers on purpose. These individuals not only established private firms in the closing years of the old communist system. They were, indeed, ready to take the entrepreneurial risk in what they perceived to be evolutionarily changing political/economic environment (on this and other expectations of "pioneers" see Horvath, 1993, and Laki, 1993). Their new goals entailed becoming the first generation of new "captains of industry" in the expected "mixed" economy in Hungary.

They clearly recognized the forthcoming opportunities and, having the needed connections to do so (as *nomenklatura*-appointed bosses of large or medium-sized state firms), they began to make the required preparations. They formulated very ambitious, usually capacity expansion-based business plans to capture the growing market shares. The main source of their optimism was that they perceived the systemic *reform* (that is "further perfectioning" of the old system) rather than the systemic *change* to the new one (shift to a capitalist market economy). They believed that the far-reaching reform of communism would bring about a much faster economic growth. And not only in Hungary, but also in other reforming communist countries.

Their ideas had been limited to what they knew, that is economic reforms (modifications of the old system). Their thinking did not go beyond the so-called "mixed" economy, in which a fast-growing new private sector coexists and in fact, more than that cooperates with the sector of reformed state-owned companies. Behind these expectations was a vision of limited political reforms. And, since they (this time rightly) perceived that economic change begins with political change, their belief in the strong role of the communist party in the modified political system suggested economic reform rather than economic change (on this differentiation, see Winiecki, 1997a).

Besides, the majority of pioneers had very good personal contacts with the representatives of the reform wing of the communist party. A remarkably high proportion of pioneers was involved in party politics at the local or national level. Given their "old tie" linkages, they expected no difficulties in obtaining, e.g., preferential loans or state guaranties.

More than ten years after the start of transition we may conclude that the pioneers' assumptions were basically wrong. Being a part of the communist establishment they did not reckon with the prospect of radical change. Change, in turn, inevitably entailed the elimination of the fundamental economic distortions generated by the communist-type economy. Elimination of system-specific excess demand meant severe transformational recession instead of the anticipated fast economic growth. And, since most other post-communist countries underwent similar systemic change, impulses for transformational recession were strengthened by the elimination of not only domestic but also foreign system-specific excess demand. Furthermore, instead of gradually evolving "mixed" economy, the rapid privatization of the state sector dominated the scene.

These unexpected developments undermined the pioneers' opportunities to benefit from their linkages within the state enterprise sector. The disappearance of the political dominance of the communist party destroyed another channel of influence open to pioneers, this time through purely *political* linkages. At the same time the increasing competition superseded the privileged position they hoped to maintain during the expected evolutionary change.

This was the beginning of their undoing. More than the half of the selected sample of pioneer-founded companies went bankrupt during the first two or three years of transition. None of them belongs at the time of writing to the group of 500 largest Hungarian firms (cf. Figyelõ , Top 2000).

Based on a case-by-case analysis of the stories, we identified typical business failures made by the pioneers. Thus, they usually tried to cover as many business activities as they could, since everything was in short supply and therefore seemingly profitable to produce. Such excessive horizontal diversification increased, however, the transaction costs and injected chaos in the decision-making structure of their firms (still fledgling, in spite of their already substantial size). The probability of failure increased as a result.

Another typical failure was excessive investment. Since communist economies were most of the time shortage economies, capacity expansion seemed be the most obvious way of supplying the market. Under communism it was important to obtain resources; paying back the loan was a non-issue. But, with the end of communism, shortages disappeared as well;

transformational recession began. Many pioneers discovered they were unable to pay back the loans they obtained so easily (thanks to the "old tie" linkages) from the still state-owned banks.

The failures in question were widely publicized and discussed in the Hungarian mass media. Criticism of pioneers concentrated upon their imperfect managerial skills and business strategy. What the critics largely missed was the pioneers' experience, acquired during the communist times, which shaped their pattern of thinking and acting (e.g. thinking in terms of the shortage economy, excessive investment strategy; symbiotic, if not downright parasitic, relationships with large state firms). It is not surprising, then, that in an early survey of Hungarian private manufacturing firms (Webster, 1992) it transpired that, e.g., the dependence on SOEs was characteristic of almost three-quarters (73 percent) of weak firms but only of one-third (34 percent) of strong firms.

What is worth stressing in the context of the numerous failures of many pre-1990 pioneers is that thousands upon thousands of newly established micro, small, and medium-sized firms performed quite well. These *de novo* or generic private firms came into being in the early transition period, when the understanding of new realities – in a nutshell: change rather than reform – became clear to would-be entrepreneurs. Their behavior was that of full-blooded capitalists, operating in a market (rather than a "mixed") economy. This was the case, regardless of the fact that their firms were of substantially smaller size than those of the pioneers (both successful and unsuccessful ones).

The performance of the *de novo* private firms, as shown in Table 4.8, proves that the new private sector (roughly similar to the SME sector) has been increasing its share in aggregate employment (and, much more slowly, in aggregate output). The share of large companies was much higher in employment in 1992 (72.1 percent) than in 2000 (44.6 percent). This development indicates that in Hungary, just as elsewhere, the micro, small and medium-sized firms are more efficient job creators than the large companies.

We have mentioned earlier that the multitude of micro companies amounts to no more than employees-turned-subcontractors of large companies in which they worked before. A large share of firms without employees belongs to that category. But a growing share of the small and medium-sized companies (24.5 percent in 1992 and 36.4 percent in 2000) shows that this sector, apart from clever use of the entrepreneurial status, created a lot of new jobs in the economy as well.

The performance of *de novo* firms (in our comparisons they are equal to all the companies except the large ones) measured by market share in aggregate output (Table 4.9) is less convincing, though. We may contribute to clarifying the picture in question in two ways.

Table 4.8 Distribution of employment in Hungary in accordance with size category of firms, 1992–2000

	1992		1996		1998		2000	
	HUF	%	HUF	%	HUF	%	HUF	%
Micro	76,686	3.4	325,870	15.2	358,235	16.7	405,747	18.5
Small	182,538	8.1	311,315	14.5	345,035	16.1	360,385	16.4
Small enterprises (incl. micro)	259,224	11.5	637,185	29.6	703,270	32.7	766,132	35.0
Medium	368,706	16.4	417,849	19.4	448,299	20.9	447,450	20.4
Small and medium-sized enterprises	627,930	27.9	1,055,034	49.1	1,151,569	53.6	1,213,582	55.4
Large	1,619 905	72.1	1,095 127	50.9	998,093	46.4	978,078	44.6
Total	2,247 835	100.0	2,150 161	100.0	2,149 662	100.0	2,191 660	100.0

Source: Computation based on 1992–2000 tax returns (database of the Institute of Small Business Development, Budapest).

Table 4.9 Distribution of net turnover of enterprises by size category, 1992–2000 (in percent)

	1992	1996	1998	1999	2000
Enterprises without employees	2.5	2.9	1.7	1.6	1.6
Micro enterprises	8.3	14.0	12.9	12.3	11.9
Small enterprises	9.0	10.8	9.7	9.2	8.5
Small enterprises (incl. self-employed and micro enterprises)	19.8	27.7	24.4	23.1	21.9
Medium-sized enterprises	13.9	19.6	19.1	18.8	18.6
Small and medium-sized enterprises	33.7	47.4	43.5	41.9	40.5
Large enterprises	66.3	52.6	56.5	58.1	59.5

Source: Computation based on 1992–2000 tax returns (database of the Institute of Small Business Development, Budapest).

The first is concerned with the specific characteristic features of small firms in the emerging market economies. They are the firms, especially micro and small ones, the output of which is most difficult for outsiders to measure. The successful tax-avoidance strategies lead many firms to shift a part of their activities into the gray economy. Micro and small enterprises have the lion's share of output in some branches of the national economy, such as construction, retail trade, real estate, etc. The fact that the share of these branches has been shrinking throughout the second half of the 1990s need not necessarily be a sign of the decreasing levels of economic activity in the sectors dominated largely by micro and small firms. It may be, by contrast, a sign of their peculiar success in hiding a part of their output – and profit! – from the tax authorities.

The second reason for the rather unconvincing statistics on performance of the SME sector during the economic recovery which started in 1997 is based on the nature of that recovery. It has been widely agreed to be an *export-led* recovery. And large firms, especially affiliates of foreign multinationals (MNEs), have been the best performers in this area, capturing the increasing share of aggregate exports (see Table 4.10).

Conclusions

The sector of *de novo* private firm thrived on systemic change, both political and economic, that has taken place since 1989. The new business climate and the clear understanding of what game is being played – the capitalist market economy game – encouraged the would-be entrepreneurs. The outcome

Table 4.10 Share in aggregate exports by size category of enterprises, 1992–2000 (in percent)

	1992	1996	1998	1999	2000
Enterprises without employees	2.0	1.7	0.5	0.4	0.4
Microenterprises	7.5	6.4	4.2	3.5	3.2
Small enterprises	5.8	5.4	3.8	3.4	3.0
Small enterprises together	15.3	13.5	8.5	7.3	6.6
Medium-sized enterprises	12.6	17.6	13.8	12.3	11.7
Small and medium-sized enterprises together	28.0	31.2	22.4	19.6	18.3
Large enterprises	72.0	68.8	77.6	80.4	81.7

Source: Computation based on 1992–2000 tax returns (database of the Institute for Small Business Development, Budapest).

thereof was a fast increase in the number of start-ups after 1989. It is only *private* firms that were established afterwards.

At the same time the understanding of the nature of change taking place in Hungary (and elsewhere in East-Central Europe) dawned rather late on the communist establishment-related pre-1990 entrepreneurs. Steeped in the old ways, they looked into the future through the glasses of the (communist) past. Old thinking cost them a lot in terms of performance.

By contrast, the performance of the new private sector has been quite good. New firms (overwhelmingly micro, small, and medium-sized ones) established after 1989 were doing very well in the early transition period and reasonably well afterwards. Their productivity was lower than that of SOEs between 1990 and 1993, but better in the 1994–97 period (see Major, 1999). Foreign-owned privatized and new ("greenfield") affiliates were more productive throughout the whole period, though. However, in terms of job creation their record is less good than in productivity growth.

True, the privatization methods preferred by the successive Hungarian governments (and, lest we forget, also by a large segment of the Hungarian public) made it very difficult for local entrepreneurs to compete for large companies. Thus, if privatized, large SOEs were primarily on offer to foreign multinationals. However, the experience of Czech citizens' privatization – by now so criticized – or, on a smaller scale, the experience of Polish employees' owned firms are not particularly encouraging as alternatives to the sale to the highest bidder.

Hungarian economy is driven to a substantial extent by large, foreign-owned firms. They dominate in exports (see above) and have a dominant position in a number of important branches of the national economy in terms of their aggregate output.

The Hungarian new private sector, that is largely SMEs, is expected to continue to dominate some branches as it has done so far and become a part of a network of efficient first-, second-, and third-tier suppliers in branches dominated by large affiliates of multinational firms. This is especially expected in those branches and product groups where the capital threshold is very high, as, for example, in automotive industries. But then no domestic firms successfully compete with global car-makers anywhere in the post-communist area (or elsewhere for that matter).

5　The Polish case

Jan Winiecki

Introduction

Preliminaries

What should be noted at the start of the analysis pursued here is, unfortunately, the *ad hoc* statistical foundations of the study of the new private sector, or even more widely defined small and medium-sized enterprises (SMEs). In spite of the importance of the phenomenon in question, its statistical coverage leaves much to be desired. There is very little in the way of regular statistics on SMEs and none of the entrepreneurial private firms within the latter.

Most of the studies of *de novo* private firms are empirical investigations pursued within the framework of various research projects with different aims, coverage, depth, and resources (with the last factor determining the varying availability of data). Thus, quantitative references and comparisons are not necessarily available for all years and subperiods of transition. Estimates and "guesstimates" are, then, an inevitable part of the considerations. Also individual researchers' preferences often dictate the subdivisions of enterprise sizes, classificational content of sectors and subsectors, etc.

Moreover, the intermittent changes in statistical classification that Polish statistics went through during the period in question make any precise comparisons over longer periods well nigh impossible. In particular, the change from the old classification of the national economy in communist times (Polish acronym: KGN) to the European Union classification of economic activities (ECA) shifted a number of comparisons from calculations to category estimates because of their different coverage of sectors and branches.

And now the last but certainly not least important comment in these preliminaries. It is not only in terms of the availability of statistics that the new private sector, or privatization "from below," has been treated as a stepchild in data gathering. In fact, privatization "from below" has generated much less political interest, controversies, and public emotions than privatization "from above." In spite of its rather obvious importance it has attracted much less of the reformers' attention. As stressed already, in the Polish transition program, announced by the government in October 1989, no more than *half a sentence* was devoted to the expansion of the new private sector (see *Program*, 1989).

Interestingly, at the start of transition it was not clear to everybody that it was only new *private* firms that would matter in the process of the privatization of the Polish economy. With so many believers, in the victorious "Solidarity" camp and beyond, in the "workers' self-management" utopia, in the restoration of the "real" cooperative movement (i.e. undistorted by communism), and what not, it was the importance of new firms, not new *private* firms that could be mentioned without an outcry.

In fact, for the same reasons, even the term "privatization" was not used in the program in question. The euphemistic term officially used from the beginning was "ownership transformation." And, indeed, the first agency that was to deal with privatization "from above" was called the Office of the Plenipotentiary for Ownership Transformation. The office was later upgraded to the level of Ministry but the term privatization never appeared in its name (to be precise it was, later still, renamed Ministry of the Treasury, again without mentioning privatization).

So, it was just as well, maybe, that the new private sector did not receive more attention from policy-makers and trade unions, the latter being very active in old state-owned enterprises (SOEs) and decreasingly active in the privatized ex-SOEs. The limited institutional efforts devoted to the new firms were enough to establish the minimum institutional framework, based on the principle of economic freedom. Add to the foregoing a modicum of macroeconomic stability that had been present from the start and increasing over time. These institutional measures and policies, however limited, were enough to free the entrepreneurial initiative of private individuals.

Private sector before "Day One"

Before transition started on January 1, 1990, the private sector in Poland was, apart from agriculture, at the periphery of economic activity, even if it had an advantage over that of, say, the then Czechoslovakia in that it existed at all. In comparative perspective only in Hungary had the non-agricultural private sector been larger than in Poland.

Nonetheless in figures its role was slightly more than marginal. The non-agricultural private sector employed at the end of 1989 1,780 thousand persons, that is 10.1 percent of the aggregate employment and 14 percent of non-agricultural employment. By comparison, the bureaucratized quasi-

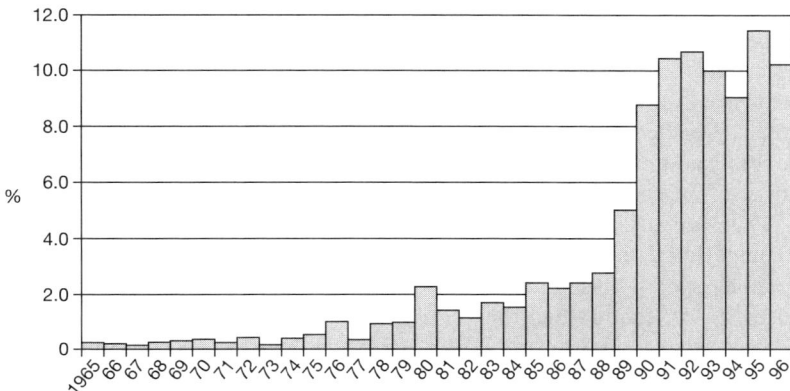

Figure 5.1 Private firms by year of establishment.

cooperative sector (which was subject to central control) employed 2.2 million persons, while the state sector employed 9.3 million.

Even that size has been the outcome of the changing climate *vis-à-vis* private ownership in the last years of communism. As shown well in Figure 5.1 the number of new private firms doubled in the 1985–89 period compared to the preceding 20 years (1965–84), see Liwiński (1998). The rate of enterprise formation doubled again in 1990, the first year of transition, and stayed at a high level subsequently, growing at a fast clip.

Private firms, including the self-employed (mainly artisans), who started on the entrepreneurial path before "Day One" of Polish transformation had the apparent advantage of experience over the owners of *de novo* firms, established after the start of transition. However, in the opinion of the author that advantage had been more apparent than real.

The corrosive legacy of the past

The start of the transition program, underpinned by the rules and policies of stabilization and liberalization which were established between October and December 1989, including some rules from the last days of communism (especially the quite liberal law on entrepreneurship of December 1988), shifted the Polish economy on to the path to a new economic system. But it is worth noting that the new market rules of the game were new for *all* economic agents, not just for the overwhelmingly dominant state sector.

True, SOEs were most strongly affected as they were caught between the peculiar microeconomic rationality, resulting from the structure of incentives for enterprises (see Chapter 1), and macroeconomic demands of central planners and their political masters. But the non-market environment, with its perverse incentives, stacked against decent workmanship, quality improvement, and innovation, as well as the perennial excess demand and shortages, influenced – or to put it frankly demoralized – all participants in the economic game. Whether managers and employees in SOEs, or in bureaucratized and centrally administered quasi-cooperatives, or private entrepreneurs: all were adversely affected by the undemanding environment in which they operated.

Thus, private firms and artisans did not need to exert themselves by trying to outperform state suppliers in terms of quality, variety, and technological sophistication (or fashion, in the case of many consumer goods). For in most cases it was enough that they simply offered their goods on the market because other goods were unavailable. A logical consequence thereof was that their goods could in fact even be *worse* than those supplied by SOEs since they did not encounter any competition. Once better SOE-produced goods were sold out, they had the market for themselves. For all those reasons it should be strongly emphasized that the "big bang," or "shock therapy," was a shock not only for the state sector but for all players in the new game.

There are neither extensive statistics nor much research to underpin the foregoing. But we may look at the study by Jackson *et al.* (1999), who had the advantage of having financed a special statistical inquiry at the Central Statistical Office (GUS). He studied certain characteristics of Polish generic private firms, cohort by cohort, on the basis of the year of establishment. Unfortunately (for our purpose), he lumped together all firms established before 1990 with those established in 1990. But even that was enough to single out the "1990 and earlier" cohort of firms in question from all other cohorts of firms established in later years.

The Jackson data concerning employment in each cohort may be taken – put simply – as a proxy of success or failure. Contracting employment of a particular cohort is taken as an indicator of failure, expanding employment as an indictor of success.

The data in Table 5.1 present the percentage loss of jobs during the 1990–96 period experienced by the cohort of firms established in 1990 and before. It transpires therefrom that very severe job losses were experienced by enterprises from all ownership categories within the cohort. Thus, SOEs, unreconstructed, reconstructed or privatized, experienced, as expected, loss of employment by 51.2 percent, 41 percent, and 34.3 percent in that order. However, cooperatives, unreconstructed or reconstructed, lost accordingly 65.7 percent and 45.7 percent of their employees, domestic private firms, small and large, lost 43.1 percent and 67.5 percent in that order, while small and medium-sized foreign private firms operating in Poland lost accordingly 45.2 percent and 77.7 percent of their employees. The percentage of firms

Table 5.1 Changes in employment in the period 1990–1996 in private firms[a] established in 1990 and earlier

Ownership	Type	Number of firms	Employment[b] 1990	Employment[b] 1996	% Loss of jobs
SOEs	Unreconstructed	3,467	3,689	1,802	51.2
	Reconstructed	5,007	1,294	763	41.0
	Privatized	935	560	368	34.3
Cooperatives	Unreconstructed	7,965	1,384	476	65.7
	Reconstructed	2,325	76	42	45.7
Private firms, domestic	Small (<101)	13,257	232	132	43.1
	Large (>100)	461	118	38	67.5
Private firms, foreign-owned	Small (<101)	778	27	15	45.2
	Large (>100)	342	94	21	77.7

Source: Jackson *et al.* (1999).

Notes:
a Excluding self-employed.
b In thousands of jobs.

from that cohort which after six years showed signs of expansion and *increased* the number of employees fluctuated between 6 percent and 18 percent of all enterprises in a given group.

This should not come as a surprise. For example, many foreign firms came to Poland in 1980s encouraged by the extremely low cost of labor (if measured by the respective costs in covertible currencies). For those export-oriented entrepreneurs it was as shocking as for SOE managers that the monthly wage increased very rapidly from about $35 per month (at the black market exchange rate) to five to seven times that, after the introduction of convertibility of the zloty on January 1, 1990.

Other aberrational distortions in the communist economy were also a source of temporary advantage for certain producers. To give but one example, Poland briefly, in the late 1980s, had become an exporter of . . . tropical flowers. The puzzle disappears if one adds that by 1989 the controlled price of a ton of coal was equal to the (uncontrolled) price of about two pounds of ham. Again, once prices were liberalized or, as in the case of coal, gradually brought up to world market levels, the aberrational comparative advantage in producing tropical flowers in hothouses heated with dirt cheap coal disappeared as well.

A more general phenomenon, namely the appearance of competition on the Polish market, also changed the rules of the game. Polish producers – be they state, cooperative or private – were forced to compete with foreign goods that for decades were absent from the market. It meant that they suddenly had to start taking care of product quality, variety, appealing look (packaging), etc. Only a small number of those succeeded in coping with these new requirements. It turned out that the experience of being an entrepreneur under communism was not much of an advantage.

Of course, the data in Table 5.1 give an aggregate picture, presenting employment outcomes for pre-1990 and 1990 established firms together. Thus, the data on that basis may cover even steeper declines in the level of activity (including bankruptcies) of pre-1990 firms and relatively better outcomes of firms established in 1990.

Later cohorts of firms established from 1991 onwards coped significantly better with the challenges of the market as evidenced by higher survival rates and a better employment record (as a proxy for expansion) in the quoted study of Jackson et al. (1999). First of all, they already observed the (emerging) market at first hand and, even more importantly, they possessed the kind of advantages that – in the opinion of the author – were more relevant than the entrepreneurial experience under communism.

There are no extensive studies, but we may asssume (on the basis of a sample survey made on the initiative of this author) that a majority of new entrepreneurs had the experience of working in the West and, thus, of learning how the market operates there. So, they had some knowledge not only of the emerging market in Poland (something earlier established firms could not have), but an even deeper konwledge of a mature market economy (or economies, as the case might be). Incidentally, this type of advantage is rarely taken into account in analyses of entrepreneurship in Poland and other post-communist countries whose people had some opportunities to interact with the West in communist times (an exception is the quoted survey by Szymanderski, 1996).

Thus, the private sector that succeeded, all barriers notwithstanding, is basically a *new* private sector, that is, the one overwhelmingly established after the start of transition. That also means that the Polish trump card often mentioned by analysts – the survival of the private sector under communism – has been of rather limited advantage in transition. Much more important has been, in the opinion of the author, a relatively liberal treatment by communist authorities of citizens' contacts with the West since the 1970s, as they gave the latter the opportunity to observe the functioning and – for most of them – also to participate in the market economy (working legally or "in the black").

Growing role of the private sector in the Polish economy: major aggregates

Generic private sector: statistical problems with rapid systemic change

The growing role of the generic private sector started from Day One of Polish transition. There are no good statistics that would establish the numbers with certainty, as only those enterprises employing five persons or more were covered by regular statistics at that time, while the smaller ones were estimated on the basis of irregular surveys. Besides, dramatic changes of relative prices between 1989 and 1990, as well as the near-hyperinflation raging in the second half of 1989, make any comparisons in constant prices even less reliable. However, various estimates stress the largest increases in the share of the aggregate private sector taking place between 1989 and 1991. The rapid changes in share between the public and private sector were helped by the steep fall of output and (more slowly) employment in the public sector. By contrast, new firms in the private sector have been growing particularly fast.

Interestingly, the dynamics of growth of the generic private sector has been distorted in the downward direction by yet another statistical change. The privatization of the national economy proceeds as a result of both privatization "from above," that is transformation of ownership of SOEs into privately owned firms, and privatization "from below," that is the establishment and growth of the *de novo* private firms.

But statistics made the picture even more confusing by adding yet another, third, way of privatization of the national economy one that I called "privatization by reclassification" (Winiecki, 1996). In order to narrow the methodological gap between inherited communist statistics and Western standards, Central Statistical Office (GUS) reclassified cooperatives from the communist terminology-based "socialized sector" to the "private sector".

On its own, such change made sense. Cooperatives are, indeed, classified in Western statistics as one of the forms of private ownership and, therefore, belong in classificational terms to the private sector. However, in the specific conditions of Polish transition away from communism this move added to confusion in two ways:

- First, it created *ex post* a false image of a much larger private sector before the start of transition than was actually the case. Distorted as it was (see above), the private sector had under communism certain economic characteristics that differentiated it from from the state sector, or as it was then called "socialized sector." Such characteristics were basically absent in the case of the cooperatives that were almost as bureacratized and as much ruled from the centre as state enterprises. With the base, that is the size of the private sector, higher in 1989, by the same token it *reduced* the rate of growth of the generic private sector, making the percentage changes smaller.

• These changes looked smaller after reclassification for another reason than the artificially higher share in the base year (1989). In contrast with the expectations of many leftists in the victorious "Solidarity" camp, cooperatives did not survive the open competition of various forms of private ownership. Many cooperatives were quickly transformed into private partnerships, limited liability companies, etc. Many other simply went bust. It was the combined impact of both these developments that made the employment in the so-called "unreconstructed cooperatives" fall by a whopping 65.7 percent between 1990 and 1996.

GUS aggregate statistics are good at best at showing the changing percentage shares of the public and private sector: from roughly 70/30 shares in GDP in 1990 to the reverse 30/70 in 2000. They are unable to disaggregate the private sector any further, though. For that very reason two special statistical surveys were commissioned, at different times, that presented some in-depth data for certain important sectors of the economy, where statistical changes did not harm comparability too much (see Chmiel and Pawłowska, 1996, and a study commissioned for the research project, underpinning this book, Chmiel, 2000). In what follows in this section of the chapter, the author relies mainly on the data established in these surveys.

Industry: the most change-resistant sector

At the start of the period of transition, industry was the largest sector in the national economy. It was also most dominated by the large firms: in 1989 SOEs employing above 1,000 people employed in the aggregate 64.4 percent of the labor force in that sector (see Błaszczyk, 1999). This distorted size structure of Polish industry began to change with the transition to the market. The speed of change in that sector was constrained, however, by the traditional characteristic of industry as the sector where the minimum required capital is always higher than in most other sectors and subsectors of the economy. But even there changes were substantial over the 1990s and the new private sector became the agent of change, as shown in Table 5.2.

The private sector's share in industrial output in 1989, including that of pseudo-cooperatives, was equal to less than one-fifth of the public sector (15.2 percent as opposed to 84.8 percent). However, if we take into account what was said earlier about the bureaucratized and centralized cooperative

Table 5.2 Shares of the private sector in sales and employment of the industrial sector[a] in 1989–1998 in percentages (of aggregate sales and all employees)

Year	Private sector total	Cooperative subsector	New private subsector	Privatized subsector
Aggregate sales				
1989	15.2	7.8	–	–
1990	18.3	5.0	13.2	0.1
1991	27.0	5.2	20.9	0.9
1993[b]	34.6	4.2	26.1	4.3
1995[c]	39.8	3.8	23.6	12.4
1997[c]	57.5	2.9	35.3	19.3
1998	69.1	–	–	–
Aggregate employment				
1989	27.3	12.1	–	–
1990	29.6	10.7	18.8	0.1
1991	35.4	8.0	26.4	1.0
1993[b]	38.7	6.5	28.7	3.5
1995[c]	49.7	5.4	36.8	7.5
1997[c]	66.1	4.8	44.9	16.4
1998	70.1	–	–	–

Sources: Chmiel and Pawłowska (1996) for 1989–93 and Chmiel (2000) for 1995–97. Aggregate data for 1998 Błaszczyk (1999).

Notes:
a Industrial sector, so-called section D (productive activity) of the EU classification ECA, includes manufacturing industry. Earlier in the old classification (KGN) it included also mining (now section C) and production and distribution of electricity (now part of E).
b Until 1991 data according to KGN, since 1993 according to ECA.
c Chmiel (1999 and 2000) regards ratios between 1993 and 1997 as distorted due to various adjustments made by GUS. Therefore, actual changes between years might have been distributed somewhat differently.

sector under communism, and its share in 1989 (7.8 percent), the share of the private sector in industrial sales was equal in reality to about one-fifteenth of that of the public sector.

Thus, if we leave aside the disturbing share of cooperatives, the new private sector's share increased, measured by sales (see Table 5.2), in early transition from 7.4 percent in 1989 to 26.1 percent in 1993 and further to 35.3 percent in 1997 (measured by employment, it increased by 44.3 percent). By the latter date the share of the public sector in industrial output was equal to 42.5 percent. It is worth signaling that in other sectors and subsectors of the economy where a high capital threshold did not establish such a strong barrier to the entrepreneurial activity the share of the state sector shrank even faster, largely due to the expansion of the generic private sector.

But even in industry the role of the generic private sector grew quite fast. Of course, the share ratios were different in different classes of enterprises according to size. The sector of *de novo* firms is basically the sector of small and medium-sized firms. Only some of them, as experience shows, increase their size substantially over time. In industry, that process is even slower, due to the high capital threshold already mentioned.

Thus, the role of the generic private sector varied across enterprise sizes. In the subsector of small firms (employing up to 50 persons) the share of the new private sector was overwhelming almost from the start and by 1994 amounted to over 95 percent of total sales of that category. By the same year it was almost three times larger than that of the state sector in the subsector of medium-sized firms (51 to 250 employees): 74.6 percent as opposed to 25.6 percent. But even by 1997 it was still smaller than that of the public sector among large enterprises (over 250 employees): 15.2 percent as against 56.8 percent.

Enterprises in post-communist countries with a nearly non-existent or totally non-existent private sector at the start of transition, especially firms of domestic origin, almost never *start* as large enterprises. Only a small percentage of them reach the stage of a large firm during the rather long process. This build-up process, let me remind readers again, is even longer in industry.

Of course, there are always such firms everywhere, and there have been ones in Poland as well. A good example may be a furniture-maker Nowy Styl that was started by two brothers in their twenties in 1992 as a rented warehouse operation in Krosno (southeastern Poland) and is now a large, almost multinational, firm producing millions of chairs, employing almost 3,000 people (one-fifth abroad), and exporting to 45 countries. But clearly the dominant role of the new private sector is seen mostly through the activities of its small and medium-sized firms.

An interesting part of the story is the role of privatization "from above" or, for a large part of the transition period, the lack of it. Comparisons made so far between the shares of the new private sector and the public sector may not have shown such large shares of the latter. In transition countries where resistance to privatization of state-owned firms was weaker than in Poland and where anti-privatization political groupings (parties, trade unions) were less influential, the relevant comparisons after a couple of years were different. The privatized sector would grow at first slowly and later faster, while the public sector would shrink accordingly (see Chapter 2 for the outline of the pattern of change and Chapters 3 and 4 for the cases of the Czech Republic and Hungary).

Unfortunately, Poland was different. Taking industry as a case in point, only in the fifth year of transition did the share of privatized firms in industrial sales advance to a two-digit number (10 percent) and, as can be seen from Table 5.2, in the sixth year it reached 12.4 percent and in the eighth year 19.3 percent: even then somewhat more than only *half* of the share of the new private sector. And it should be noted that industry is the sector where the share of privatized firms was the largest (see the next subsection).

Aggregate dominance of the new private sector

In the national economy (in fact: most of the sectors of the national economy) taken as an aggregate, the new private sector dominates. By 1997 its share in the aggregate output was 60.4 percent, that of the privatized private sector was 10.6 percent, while the public sector's share was 25.1 percent. In different sectors and subsectors of the economy proportions differed sharply, though. In some sectors the *de novo* private firms' dominance is overwhelming, in others the picture is mixed, while there are subsectors barely touched by changes in the structure of ownership.

Table 5.3 is a good starting point to such an overview. Construction and trade and repairs are two excellent examples of the overwhelmingly dominant position achieved by generic private firms. In both subsectors the share of the generic private sector exceeded three-quarters and five-sixths respectively in the aggregate sales of these subsectors by 1997. In fact the dominant position (over 50 percent of aggregate sales) was achieved very rapidly: in the case of construction by 1992 and in trade (without repairs) as early as 1991.

There are two comments that are pertinent for the sectors concerned. The first is the reminder of a capital threshold barrier that is much weaker in these two sectors. In both, leasing (of construction equipment on a temporary basis or renting trading space) remains a valid option. In fact, in Polish trade and repair business leasing became a dominant form of acquiring trading space, since most municipal authorities were as suspicious of or hostile to privatization through sales of municipally owned real property as politicians and trade unionists. Moreover, the latter exerted pressure in favor of renting the space to the partnerships and other civil law proprietorships composed of former employees in state and cooperative retail trade organizations.

Another comment concerns the competitive selection of the most efficient alternative forms of ownership. Table 5.3 shows the dominant share of sales in 1989 in retail and wholesale trade of the cooperative subsector – 54.7 percent of total sales. However, the emergence of other alternative private property arrangements changed the situation fundamentally. Between 1989 and 1993 the formerly dominant position of the cooperatives shrank dramatically to 9.3 percent and various private arrangements, from self-employment through partnerships to various other civil law and commercial law arrangements, became dominant. A substantial number of the new private

Table 5.3 Shares of the private sector in aggregate sales in 1989–1998 in selected subsectors: construction, trade, and transportation, in percentages of aggregate sales in the subsector

Year	Private sector total	Cooperative subsector	New private subsector	Privatized subsector
Construction:				
1989	32.7	2.7	–	–
1990	26.5	2.0	24.5	0.0
1991	52.4	2.0	47.1	3.3
1993[d]	84.5	1.0	73.0	11.6
1995	83.7	0.9	67.6	15.2
1997	92.6	0.5	–	18.5
1998	91.3	–	–	–
Trade[a]				
1989	59.5	54.7	4.8[c]	–[c]
1990	63.7	35.5	28.4[c]	–[c]
1991	82.8	19.7	63.1[c]	–[c]
1993	89.1	9.3	79.8[c]	–[c]
1995[d]	92.1	6.3	82.4	3.4
1997	92.5	4.1	85.2	3.2
1998	95.0	–	–	–
Transportation[b]				
1989	–	–	–	–
1990	–	–	–	–
1991	–	–	–	–
1993[d,e]	37.3	1.7	–	–
1995[e]	35.3	1.1	33.3	0.9
1997[e]	43.4	0.7	41.1	1.6
1998[e]	34.9	–	–	–

Sources: Chmiel and Pawłowska (1996) for 1989–93, Chmiel (2000) for 1995–97, Błaszczyk (1999) for 1998.

Notes:
a   Wholesale and retail trade. Since 1995 in ECA classification together with certain personal repair services.
b   Transportation, warehousing, and communications.
c   Together new private sector and privatized sector.
d   Since 1993 data in accordance with ECA.
e   Data not for aggregate sales but for employment.

firms were those that emerged from the disintegration process of former trade cooperatives.

Transportation, wholesaling, and communications, a subsector also included in Table 5.3, yields a different picture. What we observe there is a dual development of a sort. On the one hand the sector contains the biggest

Polish monopolies (or near-monopolies): state railways (PKP) and even now the partly state-owned telecom (TPSA), as well as the state-owned airline (LOT) and the decentralized, municipally-owned dominant bus carrier (PKS). Except for the decentralized bus carrier that is forced to compete with larger and smaller private companies, all the others face very limited competition on the domestic market (often due to the distorted rules of the game and/or political support for these monopolies).

On the other hand, we observe the dynamic development of private firms in those segments of the above subsector where opportunities exist: in taxi and other car-based services, in transporting goods, in bus services, in tourist services, etc. As a result, by 1993 they had already captured over 30 percent of sales. It is most probably due to greater efficiency that their share in sales was larger than in employment, which in 1993 amounted only to 21.7 percent.

There are, however, fortunately not so many subsectors that strike the analyst by their complete immobility in the period of change. Coal mining, or even mining in general, is probably the worst example. There, over 90 percent of both sales and employment was in 1998 in the public sector. The situation was no different in electricity generation and distribution (although the pre-privatization activities were more advanced in the latter). Generally in heavy industries and in subsectors and branches of the physical infrastructure privatization did not make many inroads. Within section D of the ECA (productive activities) steel-making is probably the most conspicuous case. Thus, the aggregate dominance of the new private sector hides large islands of resistance to systemic change.

The size of the generic private sector and the "gray economy"

I have already pointed out the difficulties in estimating the shares of the private sector, and even more of the entrepreneurial, new private sector in the national economy and its components, given the scarcity of regular statistical material, the survey nature of certain types of collected data, their resultant sensitivity to continuous classificational changes, etc. To the foregoing one should add other complications. To give one important example one may look at the growth of firms in the transition period. A good starting point is Table 5.4.

It presents a dynamic picture. To begin with, the number of firms of self-employed was at the end of 1989 slightly above 884,000. Table 5.4 shows that by 1998 it exceeded 2,274,000, up by 157 percent. There are no good data for civil law and commercial code-based firms, but according to Table 5.4 the number of these firms increased in 1993–98 by 53 percent from 369,000 to 567,000. But from various scattered sources we know that the largest increase in percentage terms took place in the early period of transition (1989–93).

Table 5.4 The growth in the number of firms, including the self-employed, in the Polish economy in 1992–1998

Years	Number of economic agents		Self-employed as % of the total	Dynamics of change (preceding year = 100)	
	Total	Self-employed[a]		Total	Self-employed
National economy					
1993	1,995,327	1,625,640	81.5	–	–
1994	2,120,382	1,718,381	81.0	106.3	105.7
1995	2,110,710	1,693,427	80.2	99.5	98.5
1996	2,412,023	1,949,986	80.8	114.3	115.2
1997	2,596,890	2,090,013	80.5	107.7	107.2
1998	2,842,278	2,274,494	80.0	109.4	108.8
Manufacturing[b]					
1993	312,680	255,485	81.7	–	–
1994	322,159	259,047	80.4	103.0	101.4
1995	306,032	240,954	78.7	95.0	93.0
1996	327,156	258,278	78.9	106.9	107.2
1997	336,964	263,992	78.3	103.0	102.2
1998	353,988	277,022	78.3	105.1	104.9
Construction[c]					
1993	195,807	166,483	85.0	–	–
1994	205,438	173,398	84.4	104.9	104.2
1995	202,833	169,474	83.6	98.7	97.7
1996	233,287	197,426	84.6	115.0	116.5
1997	264,987	225,756	85.2	113.6	114.3
1998	304,697	261,733	85.9	115.0	115.9
Trade and repairs[d]					
1993	877,089	739,774	84.3	–	–
1994	925,483	776,039	83.9	105.5	104.9
1995	890,368	740,423	83.2	96.2	95.4
1996	971,996	812,609	83.6	109.2	109.7
1997	1,006,696	834,814	82.9	103.6	102.7
1998	1,060,464	874,788	82.5	105.3	104.8

Source: Chmiel (1999).

Notes:

a Self-employed, either unincorporated or sole proprietors under the civil code. Co-owners in civil code partnerships and commercial code limited liability and other companies not included.
b Section D of ECA.
c Section F of ECA.
d Section G of ECA.

However, the number of firms is a less reliable indictor of change than the changes in output and employment considered in earlier subsections, as firms tend to be registered but do not always undertake economic activity or if they do they discontinue after some time without deregistering from the firm roster (Polish acronym: REGON). Various estimates have been made over the years as to the share of active firms within the register.

A consensus opinion seems to be forming that the share of active firms in the total was about 60 percent of the registered numbers and has been on the increase over the years (Chmiel, 1999). Various estimates show that the share in question moved from about 60 percent in earlier years of transition to about 65 percent in 1997. If not based on some estimation error (an alternative that cannot be excluded (ibid.)), the increase in the activity rate may be interpreted as an optimistic development. In the stabilizing Polish economy, the survival rate of new firms goes up, that is a larger share of them operates and expands from year to year (or at least in the medium-term perspective).

The overview made on the preceding pages clearly shows that, regardless of statistical deficiencies in various sets of data, the private sector, and within it the new private sector, has been dominant in the Polish economy in terms of output and employment since the mid-1990s. The share of the private sector in GDP was estimated to be more than double that of the public sector in 1998. And the *Transition Report 2002* (EBRD, 2003) recorded the increase of that share to 75 percent GDP. Also, within the private sector, the share of the new private sector of firms established already as private from the start is dominant, exceeding substantially that of the privatized sector.

In fact, these statements are made on the basis of *official* statistics only. If one adds the so-called "gray economy," the outcome enhances the larger role of the generic private sector even further. The gray economy has been the subject of intensive debates and no less frequent attempts at estimating the size of the phenomenon in question. The most ambitious has been the study *Grey Economy in Poland* (1996) by analysts of ZBSE, a joint research unit of the Central Statistical Office and the Polish Academy of Science (ZBSE, 1996). They estimated the size of the gray economy in the mid-1990s as being at the level of 17–18 percent of the then GDP. For example, the EBRD (European Bank for Reconstruction and Development) estimates yielded a lower figure of 15.2 percent in 1994 and 12.6 percent in 1995, with the size clearly declining from 1991 (the estimate for that year was 23.5 percent of GDP).

With an estimate within the 10–20 percent of GDP range, the phenomenon inevitably affects the relative share of the private, and especially of the *de novo* private sector. Thus any reestimate of Poland's GDP taking into account the gray economy estimates must necessarily boost the share of the private sector in general, and that of the new private sector in particular. In fact, *all* increase must be ascribed to the new private sector. Gray economy activities are not pursued within public firms (except plain stealing, which together with similar phenomena is excluded from the estimates). Nor they are expected to exist in privatized firms. The latter firms are usually large, and medium-sized and unregistered (and more often than not undetected gray economy activities are generally pursued in *small* firms).

The picture is, in reality, even more complex, as gray economy activities are pursued mostly:

- as unregistered activities in registered firms (hidden output, hidden employment, hidden part of remuneration, hidden profits, etc.);
- as unregistered activities in *un*registered firms or activities pursued by the informally self-employed.

Each type of activity has a range of effects, which, apart from boosting the share of the private sector, are not necessarily identical and each affects the official statistics in its own way.

Thus, the latter type of activity suggests that the official data or estimates on the basis of official surveys, *underestimate* the number of firms actually operating, including those of the self-employed. Consequently, alongside the registered but never activated or deactivated firms, there are unknown numbers of unregistered, but active firms.

On the other hand, the former type of activity affects a larger range of indicators. First, it boosts the size of output by its hidden part, and even more (given the frequency of such developments) by the scale of employment in the new private sector, especially in its largest small firm segment. Second, it raises the actual level of profits of owners and level of remuneration of employees in those firms. Third, it strongly affects various calculated efficiency indicators. For example, if employment is higher than registered, then output per person must be lower (except in cases where both output and employment have been hidden to the same extent).

The simplest and most general conclusion, avoiding the intricacies of the issue of the gray economy (worthy of a separate comparative study), is that it increases the share of the private sector, especially the new private sector. The actual figure, dependent on the selection of a particular estimate for a particular period, is less important than the fact that the actual degree of privatization of the national economy is *always higher*, sometimes substantially, when the gray economy is taken into account.

Some further performance-related considerations

The preceding considerations in this chapter set the tone for the evaluation of the role of the new private sector in Poland. In contrast with all other post-communist economies it has displayed a larger share of GDP, output, and employment than the privatized sector. It is certainly an important characteristic feature of Polish transition – and the one having significant implications for the economic growth. As demonstrated elsewhere by this author (see Winiecki, 1996 and 2000b), the balance *within* the private sector – the relative shares of the new private and privatized sectors – affects the prospects for growth of the national economy, especially in the early-to-mid-transition period.

Generalizations on this subject are elaborated in Chapter 2. To briefly recall them here, the rationale for the expectations of faster economic growth in economies with a substantial (to say nothing of larger) share of the new private sector is based on the contrast between intra-firm relations in the two sets of firms. In privatized enterprises, not to mention enterprises that are still state-owned, the owner–management, and management–employee relations have been for some time a carry-over from the communist past. Privatization means that these relations among the same people (limited replacements in the management notwithstanding) are changing rather slowly under the impact of the market environment outside the firm and owners' pressure for performance within the firm.

The reason this occurs slowly is because the same people in nearly the same intra-firm environment find it difficult to get rid of the bad habits of the communist past: lack of initiative, leisure on the job, negligence, or more widely: non-observance of technological specifications, not to mention outright theft. Even firms under the control of a strategic owner face the resistance stemming therefrom. Of course, things change over time. Management at all levels is either changed or changes itself under pressure, and employees – facing the right structure of incentives – adjust to new requirements. The foregoing takes time, though. Therefore, for a number of years – variable for different types of privately owned firms – privatized firms underperform.

The story is completely different in the new firms. There, owner–managers relations (if they are not the same individuals, as is often the case) are set right, that is in accordance with the rules of the market, from the beginning. The same applies to the relations between managers and employees. What also helps considerably is the fact that in new firms it is, in a sense, the *new employees* who face the market economy standards of performance.

I do not mean here that that new firms employ only new entrants to the labor force, although the propensity of small and medium-sized enterprises to employ newcomers to the labor force is a well-established fact (see, e.g., Liwiński, 1998). What I do mean is that even the old employees with bad habits acquired in the communist past, when they find themselves in a new work environment with the right structure of incentives, adjust much faster than in the "old comradeship" of shirking, cheating, and stealing.

Given that the larger the share of the *new* private sector within the private sector, the faster the economic growth of the post-communist economy in transition should be, *ceteris paribus*. This is especially true during the first, say, three to seven years of transition (i.e. in the short to medium term), when slow adjustment in privatized firms takes place.

The superior performance of new private firms should show up in a variety of efficiency statistics. As usual, however, problems exist with their availability and, no less or may be even more so, with their reliability. Traditional indicators of cost/sales ratio, or various profitability ratios, generally underestimate the performance of new firms, especially small and medium-sized firms, where owners-managers are better able to:

1 either include a sizable part of their own consumption into their firm's costs; and/or
2 under-report profits.

The most ambitious and extensive Polish study of the gray economy (Szara strefa, 1996) included a study containing recalculations of the level of wages, output, profits, and other indicators, made on the basis of a thoroughly analyzed sample of private small and middle-sized firms in a given region (Kielce). As a result of the inquiry, analysts from the regional statistical office found that gross wages in the analyzed private SMEs were higher by 24.4 percent, gross output by 47.5 percent and gross profits by 133.2 percent. Clearly, any corrections of the officially reported figures by the ratios established by the said inquiry would very substantially improve efficiency indicators of new private small and middle-sized firms. Since all these upward recalculations concern the *de novo* firms, their relative performance *vis-à-vis* that of privatized firms is significantly better than the official statistics suggest. In fact, recalculated sales per employee indicator had to be increased – if it were to be based on the results of the said inquiry – by 32.1 percent in small private firms and by 24.2 percent in middle-sized ones. The differential between the two figures seems to confirm that the room for manipulation of statistics associated with economic activity is the largest in small firms.

However, even without the recalculations driven by the gray economy, data on productivity measured by sales per employee point to the superiority of the private sector over the public one. In a series of studies either of aggregated groups of enterprises in the national economy, or disaggregated by the size of firms, new private firms perform better (Chmiel, 1999; Jackson *et al.*, 1999). At the lower level of aggregation, i.e. within the private sector, in the statistical survey commissioned for the research project underpinning this chapter, Chmiel (2000) was able to collect the data for a slightly different performance indicator, that is value added per employee for the 1996–97 period. His estimates (including some gray economy effects) showed the superior performance of the new private sector over the privatized sector in the aggregate for all enterprises in these two classes and for each size group: small, middle-sized, and large, for both years. The basic data are found in Table 5.5.

At the level of sectors and subsectors of the economy for which estimates could be made, only in the trade and repairs sector did privatized large firms (above 250 employees) perform better. Elsewhere, in that sector and in other sectors and subsectors, the new private firms were at the top.

For the sake of completeness mention should be made of the performance of the (vanishing) cooperative sector. In all empirical studies which include the coops their performance is very significantly below all other forms of ownership: new private, privatized, and public. Their performance indicators are additional evidence of their inferior ability to compete in an unconstrained market economy.

In the context of performance one more issue should be raised at the end of this section, namely the performance effects of foreign direct investment,

Table 5.5 Value added per employee in the national economy[a] in the aggregate and according to the size of firms[b] in 1996–1997 (in thousand zlotys)

Size/ Year	Aggregate	Public sector	Private sector	New private subsector	Privatized subsector
All firms					
1996	28.3	26.4	29.2	30.6	30.0
1997	33.5	34.2	33.3	34.8	31.4
Small firms					
1996	30.1	9.2	31.0	31.4	25.5
1997	33.7	16.5	34.1	34.5	29.0
Middle-sized firms					
1996	21.7	20.1	22.2	25.3	23.0
1997	28.1	25.0	28.9	32.6	26.0
Large firms					
1996	28.5	28.4	28.8	31.3	31.1
1997	35.5	36.5	34.2	41.7	32.0

Source: Chmiel (2000).

Notes:
a Gross value added in four large sectors and subsectors of the national economy: industry (including mining and electricity); construction; transport, warehousing, and communications; and trade and repairs.

b Small, employing fewer than 50 persons, middle-sized employing 50–250 persons, and large employing more than 250 persons.

the level of which is rising. Especially since the mid-1990s, when the international business community's confidence in the stability and dynamics of the Polish economy began to increase, the volume of foreign investment changed from somewhat more than a trickle to almost a flood (by the standards of the post-communist countries). Moreover, foreign firms radically extended their range of interests from the acquisition of privatized firms to "greenfield" investments. The inevitable consequence of this has been the growing presence of foreign-owned *de novo* firms. And, in turn, the consequence of that has been an improved level of performance by the new private sector as a whole and in all size classes of the new private firms. Contrary to the general impression that it is large and very large multi-nationals that invest in Poland, most of the foreign-owned firms and joint ventures are small and medium-sized firms.

The statistics reveal that, on average, foreign-owned firms are larger in their size category, are better endowed with capital, and accordingly enjoy higher productivity than domestic private enterprises in their category. Their productivity also grows faster from year to year. It is reflected in part in Table 5.6, which presents some of the productivity data for the industrial sector.

Table 5.6 Sales per employee in 1990–1997 in selected size categories of firms from the industrial sector of the Polish economy[a] in thousand zlotys

Size and Sector	1990	1991	1992	1993	1994	1995	1996	1997
All firms								
Public	14	23	33	43	65	85	106	142
Private domestic	11	24	35	49	64	85	104	116
Private foreign	12	19	39	56	82	127	183	222
Firms employing 21–100 persons								
Public	9	21	20	26	34	45	65	88
Private domestic	9	22	34	46	62	74	89	104
Private foreign	13	19	46	81	96	122	158	188
Firms employing 500 persons and more								
Public	14	24	35	46	70	91	113	154
Private domestic	12	21	34	57	72	99	128	129
Private foreign	12	17	28	33	59	110	196	231

Source: Chmiel (1999).

Note:

a Industrial sector in accordance with the old KGN classification, including mining and electricity, gas, and water (sections C,D, and E of the ECA classification).

Institutional environment, financial sector linkages, and barriers to expansion

Regulation of entry and business activities: a relatively free environment as a Polish advantage

I would like, again, to refer the reader to Chapter 2 (pages 53–68), where I outlined three levels of institutional framework affecting the performance of a transition economy. We observed three increasingly wide frameworks of what may be perceived as the institutional environment in the national economy. Each of them may facilitate or otherwise constrain business activities.

The first and most narrow framework would be a set of specific rules and institutions applying those rules to a particular area of activity or to a particular set of economic agents. The author will concentrate here on the more specific issues related to the first and most narrow circle of rules and organizations applying the rules and their impact upon performance. Among those the regulation of entry merits attention for obvious reasons: low barriers to entry (as well as exit) are an indicator of relatively well-functioning competitive markets.

It is not only the opinion of the author that Polish economic agents faced relatively easy entry conditions at the start of transition. The 1988 law on the freedom of economic activity was quite liberal in drawing the limits to economic freedom and regulating sparingly the behavior of economic agents. It was meant at the time as one of the measures propping up the decreasingly efficient and already shrinking communist economy. It could not reverse the collapse of the communist political and economic system (given their complete lack of credibility), but in the changed circumstances of democratic and market transition it became an important factor, integrated into the transition framework. Almost incessantly modified (not always for the better), it has nonetheless been one of the better rule sets of its type in transition countries.

A large-scale comparative study of the regulation of entry by Djankov *et al.* (2000), measuring a number of administrative and other necessary procedures, the average time of completion, as well as costs incurred, gave Poland 28–29 place among 75 countries under study. Among post-communist countries Poland's relative position was not so outstanding (fifth place), with 10 procedures, average time 26 days, and cost equal to 28 percent of Polish GNP *per capita*, yielding to Latvia, Bulgaria, Kyrgyz Republic, and Ukraine (?). The assessment is in agreement with local studies that regard Polish entry requirements as relatively liberal (see E. Balcerowicz, 1999a and 1999b). A sample survey-based study by Maciejewski and Kondratowicz (1996) concluded that almost two-thirds of entrepreneurs (65.3 percent) established their firms in less than a month, not a bad result for the region in question.

Polish and foreign entrepreneurs encountered further problems with limitations of economic freedom during their business activities. They faced a variety constraints, beginning with the requirement to obtain a license (or a similar type of permission) through time-consuming and costly labor regulations (with the labor code being the strongest, but not the only barrier), through high taxes and ever-changing taxation rules, to financial market constraints, typical for all small and medium-sized firms, as well as country-specific ones.

From increasing licensing requirements toward general over-regulation

The liberal 1988 law on entrepreneurship had been modified dozens of times until it was finally superseded by a new, more extensive and certainly not freer market-oriented law that came into being in 2001. The new law has also been changed a number of times each year, and now a new bill is passing through parliament.

Among some of the changes taking place in the law, more and more limitations had been put upon the freedom of entrepreneurs in the form of requirements to obtain a variety of licenses for a particular type of business activity. These concessions and concession-like requirements were growing in number. For example, a new, allegedly liberal-conservative, coalition came to power in 1997, promising, *inter alia*, the freeing up of entrepreneurial initiative. The "debureaucratization commission" had been created – with great fanfare – which was to prepare the set of recommendations to liberalize various rules, as well as to simplify administrative procedures.

The bureaucracy, however, coped better with the "debureaucratizers" than the other way round. Under-secretaries of state from various ministries, mostly the same people who prepared the constraining rules in the first place, were appointed as the heads of subcommissions responsible for the liberalization of respective laws. Unsurprisingly, they did their utmost to keep changes to an absolute minimum. The result was, for example, that after three years the number of licenses and similar requirements *had increased* by a third. The new law on entrepreneurship at most restored the *status quo ante*, that is reduced their number to a level existing three years earlier, that is before the attempt to change the law had started.

Licensing has not been the only area where fetters proliferated. In many situations constraints were not always put directly upon firms, but often hung over them like a sword of Damocles. Such cases have been on the increase since early transition, approximately since 1993.

They usually had two major sources. The first were the attempts of the bureaucracy to regain lost territory. In these efforts they were strongly supported by various lobbies which were also pressing for re-regulation. If bureaucrats fought for re-regulation for reasons of the general benefits to themselves (power and possible kudos from bestowing privileges in the form of licenses upon favored parties), lobbies fought for sectoral, or specific benefits.

A good example in Poland (and not only there) is the Craft Chamber. Its members, demoralized like everybody else under communism (see above, pages 128–132), lost a very large part of the market to new firms established after 1989 and to imports. As a result they joined state firms in lobbying for import controls and lobbied on their own for more regulations. They hoped that the constraints put on others would reduce the level of competition and restore at least in part the near-monopoly position they held under communism. Politically they allied themselves with others longing for the old, controlled order, becoming an institutional component of the post-communist Alliance of Democratic Left.

Another source of new restraints was the harmonization procedures, adjusting Polish business and other regulations to European Union standards. In some areas EU rules have added to the extent and/or depth of regulation of the Polish economy. In many more cases, however, harmonization has, for the politicians and bureaucrats, been a pretext to increase the degree of control over the business activity of economic agents. Many regulations were adopted that were absolutely *not* required by the EU. More – in a number of cases, as revealed during the program called Monitoring of Regulatory Initiatives, implemented by Polish Economists' Society (TEP) – expert opinions attached to the draft bills stated *expressis verbis* that certain regulations are *in conflict* with the EU regulations – and they were passed nonetheless.

The problem is that politicians of almost all colors have discovered the usefulness of regulations for both their political and their personal spheres of interest. The new alliance with the bureacracy and with special interest groups interacting with each other created a strong constituency for increased regulation of the economy. More regulation means not only more political favors (political corruption), but also more opportunities for enrichment (personal corruption). The situation is in fact even worse than that.

As stressed by this author (Stefanowicz and Winiecki, 1997), it is not only the kinds of constraints that matter for economic freedom, but also they way they are imposed. Polish law-making tradition, again inherited from communist times, has been to create empty shell-like parliamentary bills that delegated most of the decisions affecting the rights and duties of citizens in their various roles, also as economic agents, to the executive. Thus, it was not parliamentary bills but secondary rules and discretionary decisions issued by the bureaucracy that, in our context, affected the performance of economic agents. And one need not add to the foregoing that both the shell-like rules and the secondary rules drew the areas of discretion for the bureaucracy as widely as possible.

The approach to law-making briefly outlined here not only reduces economic freedom whenever the rules limit business opportunities, or add to their costs (compliance costs, bribe costs, etc.), but also raise the level of uncertainty in the economy. The consequences are higher transaction costs, fewer transactions, and a lower level of wealth created.

Two strong constraints getting stronger: labor regulations and taxes

Nobody likes taxes and Polish private entrepreneurs are not an exception. In fact, as noted on pages 139–142 in the context of the gray economy, those running small and medium-sized firms have been able to cope with tax burden in various ways, including escape with a part of their activities into the gray economy. There is, however, an area of taxation, or tax-like charges, that is becoming an increasing burden for the whole business sector: not only for new firms we are interested in here.

In fact, the social security contributions, in reality social security *taxes*, are not the only labor-related problem for the Polish business community. Let us first lay out the political framework within which the burden is getting ever stronger. The two major political alliances in Poland have a very strong trade union wing. "Solidarity" has, in fact, been the leading force of the "Solidarity Electoral Action," which ran the country in 1997–2001. At the other end of the spectrum the post-communist SLD is composed of two major union groups: post-communist trade unions and the teachers' union. To the foregoing you should add the peasants' party (PSL), which is in fact little else than a "closed shop" trade union *per se*.

In such an environment there is a constant parliamentary pressure to vote more rights, more privileges, higher minimum wages, etc., for the employees. The labor code, which is constantly being modified is extremely one-sided (the best example: extensive right to strike, but no right to lock-out) and extremely costly. Polish employees now have a shorter working week and longer vacation than in a number of much richer European Union countries. The total number of hours at work is now on the level of Germany.

These various provisions are extremely costly. Employers not only pay high social security taxes, but at the same time they are obliged to pay the employee for the first 35 days of his or her absence from work (social security administration takes over the duty to pay wages only afterwards). How one-sided the duties are can be seen from two more examples. First, an employee in search of a new job has the right to demand three days a month for the search of new job. And the right is applicable in both types of situation, namely when the employee is dismissed, or when he or she resigned from the job on their own initiative. Moreover, if it is the employee who demands immediate departure, he or she has to be paid the statutory forward wages (and employer can only claim them back through the courts).

Not only is the labor code a source of high labor costs. If we add up the social security taxes paid by employers and the withholding tax which employers have to transfer to tax offices, this amounts to almost 80 percent of the net wage. And an extra layer of regulations adds to the cost burden. No surprise, then, that since 1998 the Polish economy has not created new jobs. And that was true regardless of the fact that at first its GDP had been growing within 4–5 percent and later within 1–3 percent per year range. For SMEs, in particular, this burden has been crushing and as usual, to survive, entrepreneurs turned to the gray economy for survival.

This author guesstimates that the share of the gray economy has been on the increase since the mid-1990s as a response to over-regulation, bureaucratization, overtaxation, and corruption. This informed guess seems to have been supported by a recent survey commissioned by the Polish Confederation of Private Employers (PKPP). The employers surveyed put the size of the gray economy in 2002 at 20.2 percent of sales and 18.6 percent of employment (PKPP, 2003). The results of the survey clearly contradict estimates which suggests a decline in the gray economy from earlier years (see the preceding section of this chapter).

Through the voices of representatives of business organizations and in many sample surveys entrepreneurs have been pointing at the labor regulations (and taxes) as the two most strongly constraining factors. A survey quoted in Balcerowicz (1999b) proves the point. Among the obstacles to expansion owners and managers gave priority to the following problems, in descending order of severity (on a scale from 1: "no problem at all" to 5: "a severe problem"):

1 The high burden of taxes and social security contributions (what we call here "social security taxes"): 4.00 pts;
2 Problems related to regulation (later subdivided into frequent changes and non-transparency): 3.85 pts;
3 Insufficient financing: 3.18 pts.

All other problems were judged to be below 3.00 pts, that is between a "minor problem" and a "moderate problem."

Other more recent surveys confirm the above (see the PKPP, 2003, survey already quoted and Polish entrepreneurs' answers to the European Business Survey of SMEs, EBS 2002).

And finally let us turn to taxes proper. They are not strikingly different from those in other success stories of transition, including the other two countries analyzed in Chapters 3 and 4. But they are high enough. In a recent estimate Poland's overall tax level (including tax-like contributions) has slightly exceeded that of, among others, Germany, the Czech Republic, and Hungary (see Figure 5.2).

Clearly, a middle-developed economy such as Poland simply cannot afford to have a working year as short as Germanys and on top of it taxes that are even higher in the aggregate: not, that is, if it wants to create room for further expansion, to catch up with the richer countries of Europe. Something has to give. In the short to medium run economic growth, generated to such a large extent by the new private sector, has been increasingly the loser. The situation cannot last forever, though. Since 2002 the Polish unemployment rate has hovered around 18 percent and employment in the economy has been shrinking for years. As things get worse in this respect, the old *dictum* of George Shultz will apply here with full force: "If things get bad enough, people will do even the most obvious and sensible things."

For the moment, however, the burden is growing rather than declining. Since the period 1999–2000, when public expenditures amounted to 42–43 percent GDP, their share has been on the increase year after year. In 2003 it is expected to reach 47.2 percent and in 2004 – 47.9 percent.

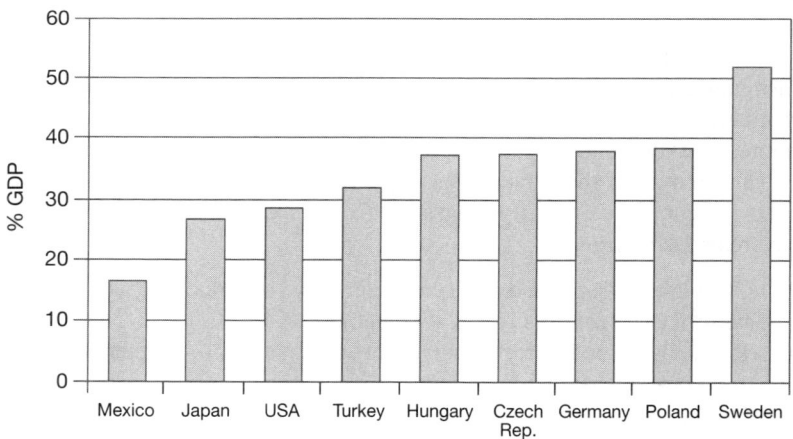

Figure 5.2 Overall tax level as percentage of GDP (selected countries, late 1990s).

Financing small and medium-sized firms: how serious is the problem?

Small and medium-sized enterprises, private or not (usually co-ops in the latter cases), have been complaining everywhere about their disadvantageous position in acquiring external financing for their firms. This is confirmed by numerous studies showing own savings as the overwhelming source of start-up capital and early financing. Polish transition has not been different in this respect. Sample surveys made at various phases of transition have confirmed the general pattern.

Two other surveys show that start-up capital has indeed come from own capital (own savings and those of relatives): the share of the latter in the total was 79.8 percent in the case of one survey (Bratkowski *et al.*, 1998) and about 75 percent in the case of the other (Balcerowicz, 1999b). The structure of financing working capital and investment also points to the relatively limited role of bank credit. With respect to investment the PKPP survey (2003) shows that retained profits are shown to be the source of investment financing in 90 percent of cases, as against 17 percent for banking credits.

Such figures usually give rise not only to complaints but also to accusations of discrimination or bias. However, a simple answer explains a significant part of the difference between the respective shares of SMEs and large firms in access to credit. Smaller firms require smaller loans. But the cost of due diligence in the loan application and later procedures of monitoring the firm, once the loan is extended, are declining less than proportionally to the size of the loan. Thus, transaction costs are higher per monetary unit of a loan and that necessitates higher interest rates (another perennial complaint of owners of smaller firms). This and other SME financing-related issues are well explained by Luczka (2001).

Moreover, smaller firms have a smaller and less varied range of assets that may serve as a collateral. For SMEs, especially recently established firms, the availability of collateral is almost an essential as a condition for a loan, since these firms have little track record, or past credit history, and this makes it difficult for banks to assess such firms' performance. Under the circumstances banks must rely to a much greater extent on collateral as a loan security-enhancing measure. And, indeed, the majority of firms that were refused credit in a three-country sample survey quoted above (Bratkowski *et al.*, 1998) gave the lack of (acceptable) collateral as the main reason for refusal. The question arises whether there are economically sensible solutions to this problem.

The most frequent proposal coming from many entrepreneurs, some business associations, and eager politicians is to make an arrangement that would supply preferential credits to SMEs, that is credits at lower than commercial credit interest rates. But again, economics reasserts itself. There is no free lunch: if some credits are extended at preferential (subsidized) rates, then somebody else will have to pay for it. It will be either taxpayers, or, if banks are state-owned and can be arm-twisted to establish such loan arrangements, it will be other bank clients. And the clients will be both other SMEs that have not obtained subsidized loans and larger enterprises. Since there is no guarantee that the firms with subsidized loans are the best performers, the misallocation of capital is almost certain.

Now, the bank arm-twisting option is almost impossible in Poland (although it was a possibility in early transition). About three-quarters of banks, in terms of own capital and assets, is presently foreign-owned. These banks are, fortunately, much less amenable to political pressures. So, the only costly alternative is the state budget subsidy. Therefore, various other solutions have already been tried over the years, often on a small-scale basis.

The most promising among them are two types of arrangements. Mixed foreign/domestic credit guarantee schemes reduce the cost of borrowing by shifting them largely onto foreign aid agencies (in fact their taxpayers). They may bring temporary relief in the precarious process of adjustment to the emerging market economy, but it is not a long-term solution (although some politicians are thinking in terms of long-term support for such and many other schemes, financial and non-financial, from the structural funds of the EU after accession).

Better, because they are based on sounder foundations, are market based solutions such as mutual guarantee funds. Such funds had already come into being in the nineteenth century in Western Europe. In Belgium, and later France, Germany, Italy, Spain, and elsewhere, business organizations (guilds, merchant associations, etc.) began establishing such institutions that, by pooling the financial resources of small firms, overcame barriers in access to and costs of financing, especially during periods of crises and recessions, when credit selection by regular banks became much tighter than in periods of prosperity.

Such arrangements do not offer subsidized credits, but they increase as access to credits offered on normal, commercial terms. In Poland such arrangements – albeit with support from external sources at the start – first began operating in 1996–97 (see Kiliański, 1999). They remained local in their territorial reach and limited in size, however.

As usual with the touchy issue of financing SMEs, there are no good solutions and Poland is not an exception. That, however, does not conflict with the following two facts. The first is that successive Polish governments have been less active than governments of other successful transition countries. And, the second is that Poland's new private sector has been more numerous and more successful than that of any other post-communist economy and its share in the aggregate private sector in output and employment is a source of envy. These two facts are clearly contradictory and the second one suggests that, probably, the general business climate – one of freedom of entrepreneurship and vigorous, lasting expansion – may matter more than specifically crafted forms of support.

Conclusions

The future of the Polish economy has been enormously strengthened by the developments in transition that, unplanned and even unpredicted, have opened up opportunities for rapid change in not only the size but also in the composition of the private sector. And it is the *new* private sector, not the privatized sector, that creates the real opportunities for quickly overcoming the effects of transformational recession which are inevitable at the start of a period of systemic change.

It is thanks to the new private sector that output began to increase so early in Poland's transition (by mid-1992). Moreover, the growing number of *de novo* business firms complemented the privatized and as-yet-not-privatized SOEs in recreating – after half a century – a healthy size structure of firms in the Polish economy.

References

Acs, Z. J., 2003, The historical role of the SME sector in developing and developed capitalist states, in R.J. McIntyre and B. Dallago, *Small and Medium Enterprises in Transitional Economies*, Palgrave-Macmillan: pp. 18–35.

A Kis, *see under* Kis

Aslund, A., 1994, Lessons of the first four years of systemic change in Eastern Europe, *Journal of Comparative Economics*, 19: 22–38.

Balcerowicz, E., 1999b, Bariery rozwoju sektora prywatnego w Polsce (Barriers to the growth of the private sector in Poland), in B. Blaszczyk, (ed.), *Uwarunkowania wzrostu sektora prywatnego w Polsce* (Determinants of the growth of the private sector in Poland), Center for Social and Economic Research, Warsaw: pp. 35–76.

Balcerowicz, E., Balcerowicz, L., and I. Hashi, (eds.),1999, *Barriers to Entry and Growth of Private Companies in Poland, the Czech Republic, Hungary, Albania, and Lithuania*, Center for Social and Economic Research, Warsaw.

Balcerowicz, L., 1995, *Wolność i rozwój: Ekonomia wolnego rynku* (Freedom and Development: The Economics of Free Markets), Wydawnictwo Znak, Kraków.

Benacek, V., 1995, Entrepreneurship in transition. *East European Journal of Economics*, 33(2): 38–75.

Benacek, V., 1997c, Small businesses and private entrepreneurship during transition, in G., Grabher and D. Stark (eds), *Restructuring Networks in Post-Socialism*, Oxford University Press, New York: pp. 209–241.

Benacek, V. and A. Zemplinerova, 1994, Problems and environment of small businesses in the Czech Republic, *Small Business Economics*, 7: 437–450.

Benacek, V. and A. Zemplinerova, 1997a, The new private sector in the Czech Republic, in M. Mejstrik (ed.) *The Privatization Process in East-Central Europe*, Kluwer, London: pp. 214–26.

Benacek, V. and A. Zemplinerova, 1997b, Foreign direct investment in the Czech manufacturing sector, *Prague Economic Papers*, June: 141–155.

Berg, A. and O. Blanchard, 1994, Stabilization and transition: Poland 1990–91, in O. J. Blanchard, K. A. Froot, and J. D. Sachs, (eds.), *The Transition in Eastern Europe*, University of Chicago Press, Chicago.

Besançon, A., 1984, *Anatomie d'un spectre. L'economie politique du socialisme reel*, Warsaw (Polish *samizdat* edition).

Bhaduri, A. and K. Laski, 1992, The relevance of Michal Kalecki today, Working paper of Vienna Institute for Comparative Economic Studies, Vienna.

Bilsen, V. and J. Konings, 1998, Job creation, job destruction and growth of newly established, privatized and state-owned enterprises in transition economies, *Journal of Comparative Economics*, 26: 429–445.

Blanchard, O., 1997, *The Economics of Post-Communist Transition*, Clarendon Lectures in Economics, Oxford University Press, Oxford.

Blanchard, O. and M. Kremer, 1997, Disorganization, *Quarterly Journal of Economics*, 112(4): 1091–1126.

Blaszczyk, B., 1999, Bilans prywatyzacji w Polsce po dziesieciu latach transformacji (The balance sheet of Polish privatization after 10 years), in *Uwarunkowania wzrostu sektora prywatnego w Polsce* (Determinants of the growth of the private sector in Poland), Center for Social and Economic Research, Warsaw: pp. 9–33.

Blomström M. and A. Kokko, 1994, Home country effects of FDI: Evidence from Sweden. NBER Working Paper No. 4639, Cambridge, USA.

Boda, D. and L. Neumann, 1998, *MRP és MBO a hazai privatizációban* (ESOP and MBO in the Hungarian Privatization), Állami Privatizációs és Vagyonkezelõ Rt., Budapest.

Bratkowski, A. S., 1993, The shock of transformation or the transformation of the shock? The big bang in Poland and official statistics, *Communist Economies*, 5(1): 5–28.

Bratkowski, A., I., Grosfeld, and J. Rostowski, 1999, Investment and finance in de novo private firms: Empirical results from the Czech Republic, Hungary and Poland, W. Davidson Institute, Ann Arbor, WP No. 236.

Brenner, R., 1990, The Eastern Bloc: Legal reforms first, monetary and macro-economic policies later, Département de sciences économiques, Université de Montréal, May, mimeo.

Bukhvald, E. and A. Vilensky, 2003, The development and support for small business. The experience of Hungary and lessons for Russia, *Problems of Economic Transition*, 45(11): 39–50.

Calvo, G. A. and F. Coricelli, 1993, Output collapse in Eastern Europe. The role of credit, *IMF Staff Papers*, 40(1): 32–52.

Cassel, D., 1992, Economic reforms in Central Europe: Present situation and future prospects in Poland, Hungary, and Czechoslovakia, Paper presented at the symposium 'Unification of Europe', Tokyo, June 1–2.

Charap, J., 1993, Small and intermediate private firms' contribution to GDP, Institute of Economic Studies, Charles University, Prague, September, mimeo.

Chmiel, J., 1999, *Problemy statystycznego pomiaru i analiza tendencji rozwojowych sektora prywatnych przedsiebiorstw w Polsce w latach 1990–1998* (Measurement Problems and Analysis of the Tendencies Concerning the Growth of the Polish Private Sector), Center for Social and Economic Analysis, Warsaw.

Chmiel, J., 2000, *Sprywatyzowane przedsiebiorstwa panstwowe i prywatne powstale od nowa w latach 1994–97* (Privatized State Enterprises and De Novo Private Firms in the Years 1994–97), Statistical survey. Warsaw, mimeo.

Chmiel, J. and Z. Pawlowska, 1996, *Zmiany w strukturze wlasnosci: sektor prywatny w gospodarce polskiej w latach 1990–1994* (Changes in the Ownership Structure in the Polish Economy in 1990–1994), Adam Smith Research Center, Warsaw.

Comisso, E., 1995, Legacies of the past or new institutions: The struggle over restitution in Hungary, *Comparative Political Studies*, 28(2): 200–238.

Csaba, L., 1996, The political economy of reform strategy: China and Eastern Europe compared, *Communist Economies and Economic Transformation*, 8(1): 53–65.

Csaba, L., 1998, Transformation as a subject of economic theory, KOPINT-DATORG discussion papers No. 57, Budapest.

Czakó, Á. and A. Vajda, 1993, *Kis- és középvállalkozók* (Small and Medium Enterprises), Magyar Vállalkozásfejlesztési Alapítvány, Kutatási Füzetek 2, Budapest.

Dallago, B., 2003, SME development in Hungary: Legacy, transition, and policy, in R. J. McIntyre and B. Dallago (eds.), *Small and Medium Enterprises in Transitional Economies*, Palgrave Macmillan, Houndsmill, Basingstoke.

Dervis, K. and T. Condon, 1994, Hungary – partial successes and remaining challenges: The emergence of a "gradualist" success story?, in O. Blanchard, K. Froot, and J. Sachs, *The Transition in Eastern Europe*, Vol. 1, University of Chicago Press, Chicago.

De Soto, H., 1989, *The Other Path: Invisible Revolution in the Third World*, New York.

Diczházi, Bertalan, 1998, *A külföldi tőke szerepe a privatizációban* (The Role of the Foreign Investment in Privatization), Allami Privatizációs és Vagyonkezelő Rt., Budapest.

Djankov, S., R. La Porta, F. Lopez-de-Silanez, and A. Shleifer, 2000, The regulation of entry, National Bureau of Economic Research, Inc., Working paper 7892, Cambridge, Mass.

Djankov, S., and P. Murrell, 2002, Enterprise restructuring in transition: A quantitative survey, *Journal of Economic Literature*, 40: 739–792.

EBS (European Business Survey by Grant Thornton), 2002, *Study of European SMEs*, Brussels.

European Bank for Reconstruction and Development, Transition Reports. *See Transition Reports*.

Figyelõ Top 2000, 2000, Figyelõ Kft, Budapest.

Fischer, S. and A. Gelb, 1991, The process of socialist economic transformation, *Journal of Economic Perspectives*, 5(4): 91–105.

Giday, A., 1998, *Kedvezményes privatizációs technikák* (Methods of Privatization with Preferencs), Állami Privatizációs és Vagyonkezelő Rt, Budapest.

Glinkina, S., 2003, Small business, survival strategies, and the shadow economy, in R. J. McIntyre and B. Dallago (eds.), *Small and Medium Enterprises in Transitional Economies*, Palgrave Macmillan, Houndmills, Basingstoke.

Gomulka, S., 1991, The causes of recession following stabilization, *Comparative Economic Studies*, 33(2): 71–89.

Gomulka, S., 1994, Economic and political constraints during transition, *Europe-Asia Studies*, 46(1).

Gomulka, S., 1998, Output: Causes of the decline and the recovery, in P. Boone, S. Gomulka, and R. Layard, *Emerging from Communism: Lessons from Russia, China, and Eastern Europe*, MIT Press, Cambridge, Mass.

Gomulka, S. and J. Lane, 1996, Recession dynamics following an external price shock in a transition economy, *Journal of Structural Changes and Economic Dynamics*, 8(2).

Grossman, G., 1963, Notes for a theory of the command economy, *Soviet Studies*, 15(2).

Gruszecki, T. and J. Winiecki, 1991, Privatization in East-Central Europe: A comparative perspective, *Aussenwirtschaft*, 46(1): 67–100.

Havrylyshyn, O. and D. McGettigan, 1999, Privatization in transition countries: A sampling of literature, IMF Working paper, Washington DC.

Horvath, Gyula, 1993, Comments, in *Private Sector Development and Local Government in Hungary*, Public Policy Institute Foundation, Budapest.

Institute for Small Business Development, Annual Reports. *See State of Small and Medium-Sized Businesses in Hungary.*

Jackson, J. E., *et al.*, 1999, The continued importance of business creation: The dynamics of the Polish economy 1990-1996, *ZBSE Research Bulletin*, 8(1): 5–40.

Jarosz, M., 2000, *Dziesiec lat prywatyzacji bezposredniej* (Ten years of direct sale-based privatization), Institute of Political Studies, Polish Academy of Science, Warsaw.

Jones, Eric, 1988, *Growth Recurring. Economic Change in World History.* Clarendon Press, Oxford.

Jurajda, S. and K. Terrell, 2001, Optimal speed of transition: Micro evidence from the CR, Cerge-EI, Prague, WP No. 170.

Jurajda, S. and K. Terrell, 2002, Job growth in early transition: Comparing two paths, Cerge-EI, Prague, WP series No. 201.

Johnson, S., D. Kaufman, and P. Zoido-Lobaton, 1998, Regulatory discretion and the unofficial economy, *American Economic Review. AEA Papers and Proceedings*, May.

Kaufman, D. and A. Kaliberda, 1996, Integrating the unofficial economy into the dynamics of post-socialist economies. A framework of analysis and evidence. The World Bank Policy Research Working paper 1691, Washington, DC.

Khanin, G., 1988, Economic growth: An alternative estimate, *Kommunist*, 17: 83–90 (in Russian).

Kihlgren, A., 2003, Small business in Russia – factors that slowed its development: An analysis, *Communist and Post-Communist Studies*, 36: 197–207.

Kiliański, T., 1999, Fundusze wzajemnych poreczen w Bilgoraju i Dzierzgoniu. Studium przypadku (Mutual guarantee funds in Bilgoraj and Dzierzgon. A case study), in R. Woodward (ed.), *Otoczenie instytucjonalne małych i srednich przedsiebiorstw* (The Institutional Environment for Small and Medium-Sized Enterprises), Center for Social and Economic Research, Warsaw.

(A) kis és középvállalkozás fejlesztés tervezett kormányzati feladatai (The Planned Governmental Tasks in the Small Business Development), 1997, mimeo.

160   References

(A) kis és középvállalatok helyzete, 2000, *Éves jelentés* (The State of Small and Medium Size Enterprises, Year 2000 Report), Kisvállalkozási Kutató Intézet, Budapest.

Kolodko, G. W., 2003, Transition to a market and entrepreneurship: Systemic factors and policy options, in R. J. McIntyre and B. Dallago (eds.), *Small and Medium Enterprises in Transitional Economies*, Palgrave Macmillan, Houndsmill, Basingstoke.

Kondratowicz, A. and W. Maciejewski, 1996, *Male i srednie przedsiebiorstwa w Polsce. Badania empiryczne 1992–1996* (Small and Medium-Sized Enterprises in Poland: Empirical Studies, 1992–1996), Adam Smith Research Center, Warsaw.

Kornai, J., 1979, Resource-constrained vs. demand-constrained systems, *Econometrica*, 47(4).

Kornai, J.,1980, *Economics of Shortage*, North-Holland, Amsterdam.

Kornai, J., 1986, The soft budget constraint, *Kyklos*, 39: 3–30.

Kornai, J., 1992a, *The Socialist System: The Political Economy of Communism*, Clarendon Press, Oxford.

Kornai, János, 1992b, The principles of privatization in Eastern Europe, *The Economist*, 140(2): 153–176.

Kornai, J., 1993, Transformational recession, Collegium Budapest discussion paper No. 1, Budapest.

Kornai, J., 1994, Transformational recession, *Journal of Comparative Economics*, 19(1): 36–63.

Kouba, K., 1993, Systemic changes in the Czech Economy, Paper presented at the workshop on European Economic Interaction and Integration, Vienna, 21 to 25 November.

Krasznai, Z. and J. Winiecki, 1995, Formal and informal constraints in transition to the market: Costs of neoclassical utility maximization, *Communist Economies and Economic Transformation*, 7(2).

Krueger, A. O., 1983, *Trade and Employment in Developing Countries*, Vol. 3: Synthesis and Conclusions, Chicago University Press, Chicago.

Krueger, A. O., 1984, Comparative advantage and development policy 20 years later, in *Economic Structure and Performance*, Academic Press, New York.

Lackó, Mária (1992), The extent of the illegal economy in Hungary between 1970 and 1989 – a monetary model, *Acta Oeconomica*, 44(1–2): 161–190.

Laki, M., 1993, The conditions for enterprise in Hungary, in *Private Sector Development and Local Government in Hungary*, Public Policy Institute Foundation, Budapest, pp. 5–15.

Laki, M., 1994, Firm behavior during a long transitional recession, *Acta Oeconomica*, 46(3–4): 347–370.

Laki, M., 1999, Industrial policy and small private business in extreme situations, the Hungarian case, in Anne Lorenzen *et al.* (eds.), *Institutional Change and Industrial Development In Central and Eastern Europe*, Ashgate, Aldershot.

Laki, M., 2000, Az ellenzéki pártok gazdasági elképzelései 1989–ben (The Economic Programmes of Opposition Parties in 1989), *Közgazdasági Szemle*, 47, March: 230–249.

Laki, M. (2001) The performance of newly established private companies: The case of Hungary. Economic Institute, MTA, Budapest, mimeo.

Laky, T., 1994, *Vállalkozások a Start hitel segítségével* (Business Start-Ups with the Help of "Start" Loans), Magyar Vállalkozásfejlesztési Alapítvány Kutatási Füzetek 1, Budapest.

Landes, D. S., 1998, *The Wealth and Poverty of Nations*, Norton, New York.

Laski, K., 1990, The stabilization plan for Poland, *Wirtschaftspolitische Blätter*, 5: 444–458.

Lengyel, György, 1997–1998, Entrepreneurial inclination in Hungary, 1988–1996, *International Journal of Sociology*, 27(4) Winter: 36–49.

Liwinski, J., 1998, *Male firmy prywatne na rynku pracy w Polsce* (Small Private Firms and the Labor Market in Poland), Instytut Spraw Publicznych, Warszawa.

Lovell, D. W., 2001, Trust and the politics of post-communism, *Communist and Post-Communist Studies*, 34: 27–38.

Luczka, T., 2001, *Kapital obcy w malym i srednim przedsiebiorstwie* (External Capital in a Small and Medium-Sized Enterprise), Poznan.

Major, I., 1983, Tensions in transportation and the development level of transport in some socialist countries, *Acta Oeconomica*, 30(2).

Mau, V., 2000, Russian economic reforms as perceived by western critics, in T. Komulainen and I. Korhonen (eds.), *Russian Crisis and Its Effects*, Kikimora Publ., Helsinki.

McIntyre, R. J., and B. Dallago (eds.), 2003, *Small and Medium Enterprises in Transitional Economies*, Palgrave Macmillan, Houndmills, Basingstoke.

McMillan J. and C. Woodruff, 2002, The central role of entrepreneurs in transition economies, *Journal of Economics Perspectives*, 16(3): 153–170.

Mejstrik M. and A. Zemplinerova, 2001, Survey of the SME sector in Czech Republic and Poland, Charles University, IES, mimeo.

Mihályi, P., 2000, Privatizáció és globalizáció – avagy az Anti-equilibrium újrafelfedezése (Privatization and Globalization or the Rediscovery of the Anti-Equilibrium), *Közgazdasági Szemle*, 47, November: 859–877.

Munich D., J. Svejnar, and K. Terrell, 1999, Returns to human capital under the communist wage grid and during the transition to a market economy, CERGE, Discussion Paper No. 29.

Neumann, L., 1996, *Az OFA munkahelymegtartó támogatási programjának értékelése Kutatási zárótanulmány* (Evaluation of the Workplaces' Support Program of OFA), Munkaügyi Kutatóintézet, Budapest.

North, D. C., 1990, *Institutions, Institutional Change and Economic Performance*, Cambridge University Press, Cambridge.

North, D. C. and R. P. Thomas, 1973, *The Rise of the Western World*, Cambridge University Press, Cambridge.

Nuti, D. M., 1992, How to contain economic inertia in the transitional economies, *Transition*, 2(4).

OECD, *Small and Medium Enterprise Outlook*, 2000, Paris, various years.

Orlov, A., 2003, Prospects for the development of small business in Russia, *Problems of Economic Transition*, 45(11): 59–68.

Pejovich, S., 1990, *The Economics of Property Rights. Toward a Theory of Comparative Systems*, Kluwer, Dordrecht.

Pelkmans, J., 1997, *The Economics of the EU Integration*, Longman, London.

Pinto, B., M. Belka and S. Krajewski, 1993, Transforming state enterprises in Poland: Evidence on adjustment of manufacturing firms, Brookings Papers on Economic Activity, No. 1: pp. 213–55.

PKPP (Polish Confederation of Private Employers), 2003, Konkurencyjnosc sektora MSP (The competitiveness of the SME sector), Warsaw, February, mimeo.

Porter, M. E., 1990, *The Competitive Advantage of Nations*, Macmillan, London.

Powelson, J. P., *Centuries of Economic Endeavor*, University of Michigan Press, Ann Arbor.

Program gospodarczy: Główne założenia i kierunki (Economic program: main assumptions and directions), 1989, addendum to *Rzeczpospolita daily*, Warsaw, October.

Pryor, F. L., 1985, *A Guidebook to the Comparative Study of Economic Systems*, Prentice-Hall, Englewood Cliffs, NJ.

Radaev, V., 2003, The development of small entrepreneurship in Russia, in R. J. McIntyre and B. Dallago (eds.), *Small and Medium Enterprises in Transitional Economies*, Palgrave Macmillan, New York: pp. 114–133.

Raiser, M., 1992, Soft budget constraints: An institutional interpretation of stylized facts in economic transformation in Central Eastern Europe, Kiel working paper No. 549, Kiel Institute for World Economics.

Raiser, M. 1995, Lessons for whom from whom? The transition from socialism in China and Central Eastern Europe compared, *Communist Economies and Economic Transformation*, 7(2): 133–156.

Róna-Tas, Á., 1997, *The Great Surprise of the Small Transformation. The Demise of Communism and the Rise of the Private Sector in Hungary*, University of Michigan Press, Ann Arbor.

Rosenberg, N. and L. E.Birdzell, Jr, 1986, *How the West Grew Rich*, Basic Books, New York.

Sántha, J., 1996, A vállalkozási struktúra változása a kilencvenes években (The Changing Structure of Entrepreneurship in 1990s), *Statisztikai Szemle*, 8: 421–437.

Saxenian, A., 1994, *Regional Advantage*, Harvard University Press, Cambridge, Mass.

Seleny, A., 1991, Hidden enterprise, property rights reform and political transformation in Hungary, mimeo.

Shmelev, N. P. and G. Popov, 1989, *The Turning Point: Revitalizing the Soviet Economy*, Doubleday, New York.

Siebert, H., 1991a, The transformation of a socialist economy. Lessons of German unification, Kiel working paper No. 469, The Kiel Institute of World Economics.

Siebert, H., 1991b, German unification: The economics of transition, Kiel working paper No. 468, The Kiel Institute of World Economics.

Sik, E. (1987): A láthatatlan jövedelemről (On invisible income), *Mozgó Világ* 6.

Simoneti, M., M. Rojec, and M. Rems, 2000, Enterprise sector restructuring and EU accession of Slovenia, Ljubljana, mimeo.

Sirc, L., 1981, Poland: The economics of solidarity, *Economic Affairs*, October, 61–64.

References 163

Sirc, L., 1990, Introduction to *The Polish Transformation. Programme and Progress*, Centre for Research into Communist Economies, London, July.

State of Small and Medium-Sized Business in Hungary, Annual Report, 1998, Institute for Small Business Development, Budapest.

State of Small and Medium-Sized Business in Hungary, Annual Report, 1999, Institute for Small Business Development, Budapest.

State of Small and Medium-Sized business in Hungary, Annual Report, 2000, Institute for Small Business Development, Budapest.

Stefanowicz, J. and J. Winiecki, 1997, Delegacje i upowaznienia dla wladzy wykonawczej: zagrozenie dla ladu rynkowego i zaproszenie do korupcji (Delegation of power to and authorization of the executive: Threats to the market order and an open window for corruption), Polish Society of Economists (TEP), Report No. 1/97, Warsaw.

Stein, Peter, 2001, Don't take home this Swedish model, *Wall Street Journal*, March 23–24.

Stein, P., T. D. Hopkins, and R. Vaubel, 1995, *The Hidden Cost of Regulation in Europe*, European Policy Forum, London.

Stiglitz, J. E., 1999, Whither reform? Ten years of the transition, in B. Pleskovic and J. E. Stiglitz (eds.), *Annual World Bank Conference on Development Economics*.

Szara strefa w Polsce: Rozmiary, przyczyny, konsekwencje (The gray economy in Poland: Its size, causes, and consequences), 1996, ZSBE Research Monograph, No. 233, Warsaw.

Szostkowski, M., 2003, *Kompendium statystyczne nt. malych i srednich przedsiebiorstw* (Statistical collection of data on SMEs), European University-Viadrina Frankfurt (O).

Szymanderski, J., 1996, The transformation of the Polish economy and Poles' contacts with the West: Research results, A report prepared for the Frankfurter Institut für Transformationsstudien, European University-Viadrina, mimeo.

Transition Report 1999, European Bank for Reconstruction and Development, London.

Transition Report 2000, European Bank for Reconstruction and Development, London.

Ványai, J., 1995, A pénzügyi szolgáltatások fejlõdése (The Development of Financial Services), *Európa Fórum*, 5(4), December: 35–49.

Vienna Institute for Comparative Economic Studies (WIIW), *Countries in Transition: WIIW Handbook of Statistics*, various years.

Webster, L., 1992, Private sector manufacturing in Hungary: A survey of firms, The World Bank, Washington DC, December.

Williamson, J., 1995, Output decline in Eastern Europe. Summing up the debate, in R. Holzmann, J. Gacs, and G. Winkler, *Output Decline in Eastern Europe*, Kluwer, Dordrecht.

Winiecki, J., 1982, Investment cycles and an excess demand inflation in planned economies: Sources and processes, *Acta Oeconomica*, 28(1–2).

Winiecki, J., 1986, Are Soviet-type economies entering an era of long-term decline?, *Soviet Studies*, 38(3): 325–48.

Winiecki, J., 1988, *The Distorted World of Soviet-Type Economies*, Routledge, London.

Winiecki, J., 1990, Post-Soviet-type economies in transition. What have we learned from the Polish transition programme in its first year, *Weltwirtschaftliches Archiv*, 126(4).

Winiecki, J., 1991, The inevitability of output fall in the early stages of transition to the market: Theoretical underpinnings, *Soviet Studies*, 43: 669–676.

Winiecki, J., 1992, *Privatization in Poland: A Comparative Perspective*, J.C.B. Mohr (Paul Siebeck), Tübingen.

Winiecki, J., 1993, Knowledge of Soviet-type economies and "Heterodox" stabilization-based outcomes, *Weltwirtschaftliches Archiv*, 129(2): 384–410.

Winiecki, J., 1995, The applicability of standard reform packages to Eastern Europe, *Journal of Comparative Economics*, 20: 347–367.

Winiecki, J., 1996, The superiority of eliminating barriers to entrepreneurship over privatization activism of the state, *Banca Nazionale del Lavoro Quarterly Review*, No.198, September: 313–313.

Winiecki, J., 1997a, *Political Economy of Reform and Change. The Case of Eastern Europe*, Nova Publishers, Commack NY.

Winiecki, J., 1997b, The transformation to the market: At high cost, often with a long lag, and not without question marks, *Journal of Public Policy*, 17(3): 251–268.

Winiecki, J., 1998, Formal rules, informal rules, and economic development. An organizing framework, European University-Viadrina, Economics Department Working paper 120, September.

Winiecki, J., 1999, Three crucial issues in post-communist privatization: A Polish case in comparative perspective, A paper prepared for The Mont Pelerin Society Regional Meeting: Transitions to a Free Society, Potsdam, Germany, October 26–30.

Winiecki, J., 2000a, Solving foreign trade puzzles in post-communist transition, *Post-Communist Economies*, 12(3): 261–278.

Winiecki, J., 2000b, Crucial relationship between the privatized sector and the generic private sector in post-communist privatization, *Communist and Post-Communist Studies*, 33: 505–515.

Zemplinerova, A., 1997, Small enterprises and foreign investors – Key players in enterprise restructuring and structural change, *Ekonomicky Casopis*, 45(10): 810–850.

Zemplinerova A., 2001, SMEs in the Czech economy, CERGE-EI Working paper, Charles University, Prague.

Index